"There's no Freudian anal, entertaining and enlightening."
—*The Detroit News*

"*Mama Drama* is a grand-slam home run hit if you want to resolve your emotional relationship with Mama."
—**Mark Victor Hansen, coauthor of the** *New York Times* **#1 bestselling** *Chicken Soup for the Soul* **series**

"A must-read for anyone who wants to improve the quality of her relationship with her mother."
—**Arielle Ford, author of** *Hot Chocolate for the Mystical Soul*

"This wonderfully written book is loaded with practical, positive, and uplifting ideas to heal and build perhaps the most important relationship of your life."
—**Brian Tracy, author of** *Maximum Achievement*

"Exquisitely sensitive...for mothers and daughters alike who are endeavoring not only to find themselves, but to gain or regain a mutually satisfying relationship with the 'other woman' in their life."
—**Dr. Ruth Peters, clinical psychologist and author of** *Don't Be Afraid to Discipline*

"The thing this book does...is explain how to paddle away from stormy seas."
—*The Dallas Morning New*

MAMA DRAMA

MAKING PEACE WITH

THE ONE WOMAN WHO CAN

PUSH YOUR BUTTONS,

MAKE YOU CRY,

AND DRIVE YOU CRAZY

DENISE McGREGOR

ST. MARTIN'S GRIFFIN
NEW YORK

www.stmartins.com

Library of Congress Cataloging-in-Publication Data

McGregor, Denise.
    Mama drama : making peace with the one woman who can push your but-tons, make you cry, and drive you crazy / by Denise McGregor.
        p. cm.
    Includes bibliographical references (page 233).
    ISBN 0-312-18627-4 (hc)
    ISBN 0-312-20421-3 (pbk)
    EAN 978-0312-20421-1
    1. Mothers—United States—Psychology. 2. Mothers—United States—Attitudes. 3. Mothers and daughters—United States. 4. Interpersonal con-flict—United States. 5. Interpersonal relations—United States.

HQ759.M423 998
306'.874'3—dc21

98-12781
CIP

First St. Martin's Griffin Edition: May 1999

D 10 9 8 7 6 5 4 3 2

Dedicated to

my mother, Viola Rutledge,
and the legacy of love, passion,
and generosity she has left me

and to her granddaughters
Meghan, Allison, Lauren, and Taylor,
may you always hold the memory
of your grandmother close to your hearts

CONTENTS

ACKNOWLEDGMENTS

In love and gratitude:

To the medical and spiritual staff at St. Lawrence Dimondale and Hospice of Lansing, for creating such a supportive, healing environment in which I could make peace with my mother.

To my daughters Meghan and Allison, for being so patient with Mommy's writing and giving me the inspiration to go for this dream.

To my brother Brad, for your beautiful essay, and reminding me that the most precious gift I could give my daughters was sharing the excitement of the life I was creating.

To my father Harley, who is relieved this book is not about fathers and daughters, for sharing your wonderful sense of humor.

To my grandmother Harriet, "Great Great Harriet" to my girls, for being such a loving matriarch in our family.

To my friend and the girls' grandmother Emma, for passing on such a rich legacy of love in your mothering.

To my friends Rhonda Hunter, Ilona Eve, and Paul Schumann, for nuturing me so well throughout the writing of this book.

To my ex-husband David, for keeping me in your prayers all these years and encouraging me in my new life.

To my ex-husband Tom, for honoring your commitments to me and helping with the care of our girls during the writing of this book.

To my friend Leslie Bakker, for believing in me and taking me on precious hikes that fed my soul and creativity.

To my friend Tomas Nani, for encouraging me to go deeper in my message and lead from my heart.

To my friend Pam Grady, for encouraging me and setting such a loving example as Noah's mommy.

To my friend Allana Alexander, for so lovingly holding the space for me to be and express the woman that I am.

To my friend Colleen Healy, for showing me, in your relationship with your mother, that mothers and daughters can be best friends.

To my friend and sister princessa Erin Thomas Palmeter, for including your beautiful, poetic voice in my text and for encouraging me to claim my power now.

To my friend Lynne Nieto, for sharing so much about mother-daughter body drama.

To my friend Mary Jo Crowley Steiner, for writing such funny jokes for the chapter headings.

To my friend Martha Kahn, for inspiring me with your life story, your unique sense of humor, and your willingness to continue to heal your mama drama.

To my friends Michael and Nikki Smorenberg, for doing research for me and inspiring me with your loving relationship.

To my talented typist Penny Munroe, for your loving encouragement and for making my text look so good.

To my computer wizard Angelo Rivera, for navigating me through WordPerfect and my computer glitches.

To Sensei Coryl Crane and my partners at North County Aikikai, for teaching me, both on the mat and off, that aikido is a way of life.

To my speech coach Mary Ellen Drummond, for reminding me to see the bigger picture, and encouraging me to give more than expected to my audiences.

To my friend Ariela Briagh Wilcox, for seeing the writer in me long before I saw her myself, for helping me shape the first drafts of this book, and for teaching me to honor creativity in my life.

To my mentor Fred Stemen, for teaching me so much about how relationships work and for keeping me focused with "No men and write," a rule I look forward to breaking.

To my friend and fellow author Joyce Golden Seyburn, for showing me flow, and encouraging me to be gentle with myself.

To my friend Mitch Yashin, for giving me such a great title for my book.

To Elisabeth Grant and Joy Donsky of Dupree/Miller & Associates, for their enthusiasm and support.

To my superstar agent Jan Miller, for believing so passionately in *Mama Drama,* and for launching my career as an author.

To my editor-from-heaven Jennifer Enderlin, for her precious sculpting of my text and having the vision to bring this book to mothers and daughters.

To the incredible women and men I interviewed for this book, for so honestly and passionately sharing their life stories, that others might heal.

When asked to write the foreword to *Mama Drama*, my first reaction was "and what's that?" Although I'm a long-time psychologist working with family issues, I still didn't get it. Perhaps this was because my relationship with my own mother ranged from comfortable to awesome. We got along, not so much because we worked at it, but more so because she was a really neat, tolerant person. Whatever I did was fine with her, or so I remember, and she possessed an exquisite sense of humor.

Also, it helped that I was a superlative child—rarely caught in my misbehavior. The one huge goof was being nailed in my junior year of high school for talking too much in biology class. My friend Teri and I went at it nonstop. By the second semester, Mr. Tritas had had it. He called my folks, informing them of my rudeness and prescribed appropriate punishments. He also told us that "someday we would be the death of him." Well, God nailed me the next day when the principal announced *to the entire school over the P.A. system* that earlier that morning Mr. Tritas had died of a heart attack. Thankfully, he left out the part about Teri and me killing him.

When my folks heard about this, I remember receiving the only maternal admonition of my childhood: "Ruthie . . . no more killing teachers." As that seemed to be a reasonable request at the time, I agreed and to my knowledge have complied ever since.

But many folks are not so lucky in their maternal relationships. Some endure an entire childhood filled with mother/daughter battles and guilt feelings that are not only destructive to their self-concept, but also lead to frustration and depression later in adulthood. Many also go on to repeat the negative interactive patterns learned as a child and relate to their own kids in the same inappropriate manner.

Numerous mothers have come to my office for help regarding precarious relationships with their daughters, desirous of making changes and breaking the cycle of poor communication, guilt, and lack of mutual respect. And that's where Denise's insightful stories, suggestions, and philosophies come in.

In *Mama Drama*, Denise carefully leads the reader through the evolution of miscommunication between mother and daughter, how hot buttons are discerned and then artfully pushed, and how disabling guilt comes to be passed from one generation to the next.

Learning to understand why your mother behaved as she did, or perhaps still does, is central to making changes in your perspective. The chapters entitled "The Never Good Enough Blues," "Mother-Daughter Body Drama," and "Last Shot at Miss America" walk you through the dynamics of relationships. Chapter 5, "The Power Illusion," provides concrete, no-nonsense techniques on "how to stop giving your power away to mother." Try them—the techniques work and can provide you with control in a relationship that may have previously controlled you.

Denise's thoughts on "Minimizing Mama Drama in the Next Generation" should be mandatory reading for all mothers. While reading the chapter, I found areas where I had to admit a big "Uh-oh, I'm doing this to my own kids!" Over-protecting, subtle guilt provocation and yes—the big one—"Look at how I sacrifice for you!" How easy it is to fall into the drama, yet how difficult to repair it.

And finally, I thought that I had adequately dealt with the emotions of losing my own mother several years ago, that is, until I read "Facing Your Mother's Death." In an exquisitively sensitive fashion, Denise provides realistic suggestions on how to make the last moments perhaps the best moments. Although there's no going back and undoing hurts, miscommunications, and perhaps long absences in the relationship, she shows us how forgiveness sets us free to love and to understand those who have passed on, as well as how to bestow these gifts upon our own children. This is a must-read for mothers and daughters alike who are endeavoring not only to find themselves, but to gain or regain a mutually satisfying relationship with the "other woman" in their life.

Ruth A. Peters, Ph.D.
Clinical Psychologist, and author of
Don't Be Afraid to Discipline

PART ONE

THE WOMAN

The One Woman Who Can Push

Your Buttons, Make You Cry, and

Drive You Crazy

Our mothers ought to know how to push our buttons—

they were the ones who installed them.

— LYN ELLEN

There is nothing like a visit from your mother to push your buttons. To say the least, it's an endurance test dodging the bullets of guilt, criticism, and control.

At first you look forward to seeing her. You fool yourself into believing this time things will be different, and she will somehow mysteriously become the mother you always wanted. You tell yourself you really have missed her and secretly hope to find your fantasy mother, a nineties version of June Cleaver, waiting by the curbside.

Then reality hits you like a cold shower when you pick her up at the airport and all she can talk about is how late you are and how long you made her wait with her luggage. She reminds you she's "an old woman now," and you shouldn't make her suffer in the heat and humidity. Shame on you for almost killing your mother.

"Be careful with that bag," she scolds, "I have all my cosmetics in there," as if you've never traveled yourself and schlepped your cosmetics anywhere. Then she gives you the look, that stare that only she can do, that makes you feel eight years old again, and tells you, "You look pretty good for a middle-aged woman. Is that a new hair color you're trying?" All this before you've even loaded her luggage into the car.

If you manage to get calmly in the driver's side and not look in the rearview mirror at your hair, you have more strength than most of us. But wait, this is just the beginning.

She no sooner steps foot in the door when she comments, "Your house looks good for a change." Ok, so you're not Martha Stewart and have never claimed to be. What does she mean by that comment? you wonder. You shake it off and tell yourself it doesn't matter, when your two-year-old daughter comes screaming stark naked from the bathroom followed by the dog, who has somehow managed to jump in the bath with her. "You better get control of that girl," she warns you. "Today it's rebellion in the bathtub—tomorrow it's wheelies on the front lawn." You think, Thanks, Mom, for sharing, and set off in search of the baby-sitter you thought you hired so you could calmly pick up your mother and avoid this chaos.

You check your messages only to find that your husband, bless his heart, has decided to take a "boys' night out" in honor of your mother's first night in town, so you and your mother can have "quality time" together, a lame excuse if ever there was one. At this point, you pour yourself a glass of wine, open a bag of party mix, and begin munching, just as the baby-sitter comes into the kitchen. You decide to forget the bath episode and beg mercy for extra hours so you don't have to be alone with your mother. You take another sip of wine, glance over at the calendar, and think, Only six more days until she leaves.

An Epiphany

You don't have any relief from this ongoing drama until that evening, when you see your mother cuddling with your daughter, stroking her hair, reading her a bedtime story, and singing her the same lullaby she sang you. It's the first time all day you took a good look at her as a woman, as a grandmother, and saw her as someone other than the one person who can wreak havoc with your life. You begin to cry, as you understand that there's more to this mother-daughter stuff than you ever realized. If you had stayed in the kitchen and polished off that second piece of cheesecake, you just might have missed it.

You well up with all sorts of mushy feelings and realize that you can't blame this on the wine—you're genuinely having one of those moments, those epiphanies that cut through the drama and remind you there is something redeeming about your mother after all. "Gosh, I love this woman," you think. "Why can't it be like this all the time?"

So you decide to try something bold, to curl up on the couch and listen to your mother, to exchange stories like girlfriends and see where that leads, to surrender and enjoy her no matter what she says, no matter how scary it seems. Maybe you'll even try this without your hand in the M&M jar.

Even if this bold new move doesn't immediately get you the relationship you want, it is a step in the right direction. It is seizing the fleeting moment of intimacy you saw your mother and daughter sharing, and making it your own, by sharing your own special moment with your mother.

When it comes to a relationship with our mothers, we may find ourselves choking on the drama, but wanting so much more. We cannot force our own personal epiphanies, but rather must remain open to them happening along the way. And when they do happen, we can take full advantage of the openings they create to get us closer to the relationship we want.

We would like our mothers to have the magical insight first, so they would somehow make our job as daughters easier. But chances are that won't happen. If we are the ones with the insight, then we must do the changing by attuning ourselves to that insight and setting our course from there. When we create the place for the relationship we've always wanted, our own miracles can drop in.

What Is Mama Drama?

- Can your mother make you feel guilty in thirty seconds or less?
- Do you feel that whatever you say or do, you're still not good enough for her?
- Are you coping with your mother by feeding your face or dieting with a vengeance to avoid looking like her?
- Are you putting your life on hold to live your mother's dreams for you instead of your own?
- Do you act like a grown-up in the real world but become eight years old around your mother?
- Are you letting your mother interfere in your marriage?
- Are you and your mother sounding just like your mother and grandmother did when they fought?
- Are you passing on the same sense of drama to your children?
- Are you caught in the dilemma of fearing your mother's death but not knowing what to say to her in the meantime?
- Does your mother push your buttons so much that it's hard to find anything positive about her?

If you can answer yes to one or more questions, you are experiencing *mama drama,* the ongoing conflict with your mother that never seems to go away and is often perpetuated from generation to generation.

Mama drama has *an element of addiction* to it: you may find yourself attracting both women and men in your life that can give you the same "juice" your mother did. Mama drama has *an element of isolation* to it: you may somehow feel alone in your conflict, convincing yourself that your mother is worse than all the rest. Mama drama has *an element of pervasiveness* to it: it can spread to all your relationships, to your spouse, your children, your father, even your coworkers and friends. Mama drama has *an element of resentment* in it: you may resent others who have good relationships with their mothers and appear to be living their lives more calmly. Mama drama has *an element of hopelessness* in it: you may feel drained and trapped in a downward spiral, with no hope of creating the relationship you want.

Ironically, there is an overwhelming sense among us that this is simply what mothers and daughters do. So we find ourselves stuck in conflict not only with our own mothers but also with the negative patterns perpetuated by our grandmothers and all the mothers in our family tree. And until we realize this and take steps to live outside the drama, we recreate mama drama with our own daughters, living out life scripts that were written long before their births.

Nike picked up on this *generational dysfunction* in one of their ad campaigns:

> YOU DO NOT HAVE TO BE YOUR MOTHER unless she is who you want to be. You do not have to be your mother's mother, or your mother's mother's mother, or even your grandmother's mother on your father's side. You may inherit their chins or their hips or their eyes, but you are not destined to become the women who came before you, you are not destined to live their lives. So if you inherit something, inherit their strength. If you inherit something, inherit their resilience. Because the only person you are destined to become is the person YOU DECIDE to be.

The message in the ad underscores the importance of understanding just what it is that we want to inherit from our mothers and grandmothers before us—the drama or the strength?

I'm part of the Baby Boomer generation and we Boomer daughters have grown accustomed to bucking our mothers. They were, after all, part of the Establishment. But we have become painfully aware that unless we alter our own paths, we will pass on the same legacy to our daughters, and since we like to think we've done everything better than the generations before us, that simply is not acceptable. We didn't fight for liberation only to enslave our daughters further. It's time we wake up and seize the destiny Nike refers to and create the relationship we've always wanted.

Stuck in Dead-End Solutions

I was once in a seminar with Tony Robbins when he defined insanity as "doing the same things over and over again and expecting different results." That's exactly what happens to us when we keep on trying the same old tired tactics with our mothers, naïvely hoping for different results. We may stay on the phone with her for hours, thinking that she will surprise us and magically change. But then she hooks us with one comment and we're back in high drama, fighting with her again.

So instead we may turn to our favorite radio talk-show psychologist and ask for some tough advice about how to cope with our mother. That tact prompts us to invite her to lunch and talk lots of psychobabble to her, to which she replies, "I never tried to change my parents, and you're not going to change me." How do we argue with that?

Next we try telling our mother what we don't want in the relationship, only to to get more of what we don't want. In desperation we try something that worked for one of our girlfriends only to find out that it flops miserably with our own mother. Before long we are more frustrated than ever that our efforts aren't moving us in the direction of the relationship we truly want. That's when it dawns on us that we must stop trying the same dead-end solutions and find some new options.

We realize we can't get stuck on one right answer or what might have worked for some other woman. Instead, we must focus on the relationship we want with our mother and build it in small steps, while remaining open to those experiences that drop in. They may indeed be miracles as some of us have experienced them, but they may also seem more like small blessings. They may come to us through another person or a special passage of words that speaks just to us. They may come to us as a feeling or action led by our intuition, or in some other form altogether. If we stay committed to the belief that we can have what we want, we will find our own best solutions.

One woman found peace in interviewing her mother for a class assignment. She had to go to great lengths to track her mother down, as they had been estranged from one another for years. Yet this simple, nonthreatening interview was the basis for her feeling true compassion for her mother and creating a new relationship with her.

Sitting with the Question, "What Kind of Relationship Do I Want with My Mother?"

The more we try to force a solution, the more it may escape us. In martial-arts training, we learn a concept called *sitting with the question*. It means: Instead of rushing in with the mind to find a solution, we ponder the question and allow multiple solutions to come to us.

Certain questions can take us down a dead-end path. If we are stuck wondering, "Why can't my mother change?" or "Why can't my mother love me?" we may never find our way out, because the focus is on her, not on us and what we want. At this point, we have to realize that we can't change our mothers and must stop trying to fix them.

That is the problem with some forms of therapy that keep us stuck replaying the past and analyzing our mothers through psychological classifications. How does this really help us with the day-to-day relationship with our mothers? History is incorrectable—we can only deal with the here and now. Therapy has its place, but we can spend a lifetime and thousands of dollars trying to find closure on the past with our mothers, only to discover it would have been more productive to create what we want now one step at a time. One of my friends put it this way: "I started to go to a therapist—it was expensive, and I didn't want to commit the money, because I thought I'd be marinating in the problems and nothing would get any better." Most of us have marinated in the problems long enough. It's time we ask the right questions that will lead us to the solutions that work for us.

What are the right questions? The ones that get us what we want. We can't hit a target until we know what the target is. So if we sit with the question "What kind of relationship do I want with my mother?" our subconscious will begin to reveal insights and solutions to us. If we will allow it, those solutions will come to us like beautiful shells tumbling and dancing in waves of unconditional love until one day, we are finally ready to let go, to stop blaming our mothers for ruining our lives, and create something better for ourselves and our children.

If we begin with this end in mind, that we want to create the relationship we've always wanted and the peace that comes with it, the right solutions will present themselves to us. It may be as simple as a Hallmark card that opens up the floodgates of forgiveness. It may be staring back at us in the form of our own daughter's eyes.

Creating the relationship we want with our mothers is one of the most important rites of passage into full womanhood, right up there with giving birth to our own children. We will never be all we can be until we cross the threshold of fear and face who we are in relationship to these incredible women who have had such lasting input on our destiny.

In this regard, we are our own gatekeepers, the ones who hold the keys to our destiny. Will we hold back, stay outside the gate, and fearfully wait to confront our relationship? Or will we boldly step through? The choice is ours.

It's our journey, one that only we can take. Once we pass through and reach the other side, we may wonder why we waited so long. It doesn't matter if you're a teenager hating life with your mother or if you're a woman who's lived your whole life in your mother's shadow—the relationship you want is already there waiting for you. You just need to come forward and claim it.

There is plenty of "how to" in this book, and yet what I sincerely hope is that my suggestions for a better mother-daughter relationship will guide and inspire you to find your own soulful solutions, solutions born of joy and pain that make sense for you, solutions that truly work, solutions that are consistent with who you are.

Mama Drama Guides You in Creating Your Own Soulful Solutions

Healing mama drama is different for every woman. The solution doesn't come in the busy hectic lives you may lead, but in the quiet moments. In the words you leave unspoken. In the flashes of true compassion for this woman you call Mother, Mom, or Mama. In the boldness of letting go. In the shared ritual of a lullaby or a bedtime story or the silence of sitting at your mother's bedside and facing her death.

To guide you in creating your own soulful solutions, **Mama Drama** provides several approaches: *"Try This" exercises*, real-life scenarios and suggestions for handling your mother, *Mama Drama Minutes,* confessions from your author that give insight into the drama and the peace, *interviews* of women sharing their direct experience of resolving mama drama, *techniques from hypnotherapy*, and *principles from the martial art aikido.*

In the "Try This" exercises, you will learn ways to put your new relationship with your mother into practice. In reading the Mama Drama Minutes and interviews, you may find your own voice to stand up to your mother and build a new relationship. In hypnotherapy, you will discover methods to address your "fight or flight" response that will immediately quiet your anxiety level and get you back on track. And in aikido, you will learn how to blend with your mother's resistance, redirect it, and neutralize its effect on you.

AIKIDO

Dr. John Welwood, author of *Journey of the Heart* (HarperPerennial), defines aikido as "a nonaggressive martial art that involves moving, almost dancing, with what comes to us, rather than pitting ourselves against it."

Students work in pairs—*uke* the attacker, and *nage* the defender—practicing techniques to resolve conflict. When faced with an attack, the student learns to blend with the opposing energy, extend or redirect it, and neutralize her attacker. The defender is not a victim, but one who is empowered by the techniques and staying in her center, to neutralize the attack.

Practicing this art over an extended period of time strengthens a woman's ability to stay centered and calm in the face of all conflict and controversy. Understanding the principles of this martial art gives you one more tool for better handling conflict with your mother.

The Journey of Healing Mama Drama

Mama Drama is divided into three parts. We've already started with **Part One: The Woman.** By now, you should at least have a little more understanding of your mother and the course we are setting, namely the relationship you truly want with her. In **Part Two: The Conflict**, you will explore various pitfalls and traps that interfere with your having the relationship you want with her right now. In **Part Three: The Peace**, you will learn about creating a new emotional legacy with your mother and your children.

Throughout this journey you will reconnect with deeper parts of yourself and finally accept the fact that you are your mother's daughter after all, and this thought won't seem so scary to you. You will laugh, cry, and gain new appreciation and compassion for your impossible mother, who—at the end of your journey—may not seem so impossible after all. At first you may miss the drama, but you will learn to live without it. And you may find, to your surprise, that the peace and joy you wanted was there all along, waiting for you to discover it, like a precious jewel hidden in the conflict.

Sometimes women come up to me and almost apologize. "I have a wonderful relationship with my mother." To which I reply, "Great!" They quickly follow it up with, "But my sister really fights with my mother," or "I know a girlfriend who could really use your book." It's as if they're trying to reassure me that my topic is still alive and well. They don't have to convince me. I still hear the war stories in the locker room!

And they don't have to apologize for peace with their own mothers. That's exactly why I'm writing this book, to tell women that it is possible for mothers and daughters to drop the drama and have the relationship they've always wanted now, instead of waiting for that all-looming deathbed experience.

I am a trained mental-health professional, and yet my best credential is this: I am a daughter who fought with her mother most of her life and healed her *mama drama* in the last six weeks of her mother's life. And that healing has made all the difference.

It may have been an eleventh-hour situation for me, but I am convinced that you don't have to wait. You can do the same thing right now. So relax and enjoy this book. The relationship you want is closer than you think.

PART TWO

THE CONFLICT

Mother: The Best Travel Agent

for Guilt Trips

My mother would have made a great collection agent.

She'd get you on the phone and say, "Good little girls

make their car payments. Your mother must be

ashamed of you." We'd all pay up.

Our Mothers' Two Favorite Words

Singer and comedienne Martha Kahn finds her mother's guilt trips good material for her one-woman show, "Yes I Kahn." Dressed in a dramatic black dress with matching leopard accessories, she teases, "My mother's two favorite words were 'You're wrong'." Judging from the laughter in the audience, Martha's mother wasn't the only mother who had those two words down pat.

I remember a girlfriend of mine once telling me about her mother's guilt trip at her first wedding. My friend was only nineteen years old, about to walk down the aisle, when she realized she was making a terrible mistake and couldn't go through with the wedding. Her intuition had told her in a split second that she was marrying the wrong man, and she needed to stop the ceremony. When she found her mother and told her about her decision, her mother replied, "But I've already paid for everything."

That was it, no more discussion, and my girlfriend marched down the aisle to marry Mr. Wrong because she didn't want to disappoint her mother. Try as she could, she didn't have the courage to buck her mother at her own wedding. Too bad her wedding was before the movie, *The Graduate.* Like Elaine, she needed to bolt out of that church and leave her mother and the other relatives gasping for air. It was, after all, her life.

Today I think about how incredibly brave my friend was even to risk her mother's love and approval in such a public arena. She actually did know what she wanted, but because her mother had laid a guilt trip on her, she didn't trust herself. At least she tried. I know many women much older than nineteen who would never take the risk of confronting their mothers because the stakes of losing their mothers' love are simply too high.

Guilt is the regretful awareness that we have done something wrong. Defining it in mother terms, it is the awful feelings we get after disappointing our mother or failing to do things her way. No matter how hard we try, we can't just intellectually dismiss guilt or rationalize it away, because it hits us at the core of who we are.

All it takes is one look, one comment, and we are reduced to kids again. A radio talk-show host in San Diego confided that sometimes when she talked to her mother, she felt like she was thirteen years old again. I told her we wish we could be thirteen around Mother . . . at least teenagers are rebellious. Most of us feel like seven- or eight-year-olds, helpless to defend ourselves against our mother's words.

So how do you know if you're buying into one of your mother's guilt trips? There are some important warning signals:

- You're afraid to confront your mother for fear of losing her love or approval.
- You're obsessing all the time over "what your mother will think" about a certain decision or person in your life.

- You're living out frequent dramas of conflict and remorse with your mother.
- You feel like you've done something wrong or let your mother down.
- You feel like you owe your mother, like you should do something to make her happy.
- You feel hopeless or powerless to take charge of your life.

What flaw do all these characteristics have in common?—Focus. Guilt only works when you put the focus on your mother, what she wants, what makes her happy, what she must think of you. It doesn't work so well when you put the focus on yourself, on taking those actions that make you happy and move your life forward.

Women are so used to being nurturers of others that they often feel guilty going for what they want because they feel it's selfish. This certainly comes into play with our mothers. Whereas little boys are often encouraged to separate from their mothers, go out in the world, and make their mark, little girls are raised to stay back with their mothers, with the expectation that they will one day take care of not only their own family, but of their aging parents. This is slowly changing, but the different role expectations are still there.

MAMA DRAMA MINUTE

I must admit I sprang the news on my parents with all the subtlety of a bull in a china shop. I guess I was too afraid to sit down and calmly discuss it with them. As I was unpacking my suitcase in the living room, I blurted out, "I bought this wedding dress on my trip and I'm getting married in July!" At the time they'd never met my fiancé, and now I was telling them I was moving away for good. My mother was so shocked all she could say was, "But you're supposed to stay here and take care of me in my old age." It never occurred to her that I, her daughter, might be the one to move away and claim a life of my own.

Daughters can therefore feel a dilemma most sons do not, namely, that they're abandoning their mothers to move their own lives forward.

This can be even more significant if the daughter is being raised by a single mother, because the daughter will feel there is no one else, like a husband, to help her mother out.

DRAMA TRAP: OWING YOUR LIFE TO YOUR MOTHER

The ultimate guilt trip your mother can use is robbing you of your life by instilling in you a sense that you owe her.

Before you can release this stronghold guilt over your relationship with your mother, you must understand a few more basics:

- Mother was your primary caretaker, your first love object. She taught you how to love in all other relationships.
- You have a primal need to stay connected to your mother for love and comfort, a sense of security.
- Because your mother's love nurtured your very life, risking that love (and approval) feels like life or death.

I get upset when women are advised to cut off their relationships with their mothers, because I know that this posture flies in the face of a daughter's primal need to stay connected to her mother, no matter how impossible her mother may be. Because the daughter defines herself so much through her mother, she needs to maintain a relationship with her mother to feel secure about herself and her life.

It's the knowing that her mother is there, not the amount of contact, that is the most important factor. Her mother may live three thousand miles away. She may only see her mother once or twice a year and hardly talk to her on the phone, but she still knows she's there and their connection is alive. She may be a very independent woman who never asks her mother for advice, but just knowing that she can ask her gives her some security, because she has open access to her mother. It may be an illusion of security, but it still makes her feel secure and gives her a basis for interacting with herself and the outer world.

Notice that I am not talking about another dynamic, namely the mother-daughter relationships where mother and daughter spend so much time together, they are practically joined at the hip like Siamese twins. It's great to be best friends with your mother, but if you are spending most of your time with her, at the expense of your other relationships, this won't serve you in the long run. You may find yourself giving up too much of yourself and your dreams to be buddies with your mother and resenting it later.

When a daughter goes to the opposite extreme and cuts her mother out of her life, she will either feel like she's abandoned her mother or her mother has abandoned her, and this alone will put her in a mild anxiety state, where she will feel insecure and unstable. She may also feel loss and grief as she experiences the breakup with her mother as a minideath of sorts. She may tell herself it doesn't matter, even put on a good show of it to the outside world, but inside she knows she can never fully cut her mother out of her life, and she will feel upset because of it.

What is the solution then?—finding the balance between being joined at the hip and cutting your mother out of your life. It's creating a fluid relationship that can maintain the connection and allow for visits and sharing, while still giving you breathing room to live your own life.

In aikido, we refer to this connection as a *sticky grip*, a grip that is tight enough to maintain the connection with our partner and feel where she is moving, but loose enough so we don't cut off the circulation. We can always tell the newer students on the mat, because they have the tightest grips and we come away with bruised wrists. The most experienced *senseis* (teachers), on the other hand, are the ones who have the softest grips with the greatest sense of connection.

When it comes to our mothers the same principle applies. We want to be connected enough to know where we are both moving in the relationship, but flexible enough to change direction, to disengage when necessary.

How Guilt Works

Guilt has a cycle which plays out in our lives. It starts with *expectations* (of ourselves and others), followed by *perceived failure* of those expectations, with *an emotional hook* (a look, a word, phrase) to start the guilt rolling, followed by *remorse* (self-blame, shame, disappointment) over our perceived wrongdoing, and *punishment* of ourselves and others.

Using the example of my friend's wedding again, we see that her mother's expectations were to give her daughter a beautiful day shared with family and friends (nothing evil here . . . she wanted the best for her daughter) and when her mother perceived that canceling the wedding would somehow reflect on her or her daughter as *embarrassment or failure,* she was upset and held fast to the status quo (proceeding with the wedding as planned).

Her mother's emotional hook was the phrase, "But I've already paid for everything." This set the guilt in motion by talking about money and making my friend feel like she owed her mother. It was actually my friend's fear of disappointing her mother and costing her money that caused her to go along with the marriage. But later she felt remorseful about her decision, blamed herself for not following her initial intuition, and was angry at her mother for not supporting her, which was her way of punishing her mother.

Expectations are a setup for perceived failure in our relationship with our mother and the guilt feelings we feel afterward. In the women I interviewed who experienced the most conflict with their mothers there was a recurring theme of high, unrealistic expectations. They all expected their mothers to be someone other than the women they were. And here is an interesting paradox: we are often mad at our mothers because we think we don't live up to their standards, when in fact, they don't live up to ours. We can be the ones with the tougher expectations.

Is adjusting our expectations easier said than done? You bet. We live in a society where more is better, and it's hard not to get caught up in a feeding frenzy of hope and expectations for the good life. We have a sense of entitlement in America that we should have everything we want when we want it. Why should we think, then, that these expectations should be any less intense when they apply to each other?

To move from these impossible expectations, we need to see each other for who we really are, multifaceted women with a variety of qualities rather than one-dimensional stereotypes.

> Mothers are not the nameless, faceless stereotypes who appear once a year on a greeting card with their virtues set to prose, but women who have been dealt a hand for life and play each card one at a time the best way they know how. No mother is all good or all bad, all laughing or all serious, all loving or all angry. Ambivalence runs through their veins.
> —Erma Bombeck, *Motherhood: The Second Oldest Profession*

Ambivalence is the perfect word to describe mother-daughter relationships, because it means the simultaneous holding of conflicting feelings about each other, and that is what we mothers and daughters do best. So much of our conflict comes from trying to balance the love-hate feelings we have for each other. Failure to understand this ambivalence keeps us at the mercy of our expectations. It's as if we hold each other hostage to our expectations and refuse to let go.

In my aikido practice my sensei is constantly reminding me to let go and allow myself to follow the movement instead of my expectations. As she explains it, we can actually get hurt worse moving where we expect our partner is taking us, because we can open ourselves to a different attack or move. Our anticipation or expectation of the event can actually put us in a more vulnerable position.

The same principle applies to our mothers. Moving with each other according to our expectations may put us in a more vulnerable position to experience guilt. We are better off dropping those expectations and staying close to the movement (what is happening now with our mothers) to avoid setting ourselves up for pain and conflict.

Taking the time to nurture ourselves and understand who we are, what we want, and what our dreams are is vital to our ability to move with our mothers. Otherwise, it can feel like we are ships adrift, being pulled by our mothers' expectations on us.

The tragic truth is we can live our whole lives feeling guilty or mad at our mothers, like we've disappointed them in some way, only to find out that the real person we let down was ourself, because we didn't listen to our own voice. And because we internalize our mothers' high expectations of us, we become our own worst taskmasters, driving ourselves harder and harder toward being good, obedient daughters.

Remember what Mae West said about being good: "When I'm good, I'm good . . . but when I'm bad, I'm very good." Too much compliance with our mothers' expectations, too much dying to our own will, because we're afraid to confront our mother, carries a big price to our self-esteem and freedom, and invites rebellion. It's as if our soul can't stand it anymore. . . . Either we confront our mothers or we're confronted with our own rebellion, whatever form that takes.

Joanne's Story:
Doing What Her Mother Wanted

Because Joanne's mother had buried a husband and a son, she was extra protective of her daughters, especially Joanne, who was born shortly after her brother died. Joanne felt the same sense of protection toward her mother, because she was a widow and wasn't coping well with being a single mother.

Joanne's mother shelved her own love life and set about the task of making sure Joanne married well. "In my family," Joanne confided, "my mother held me up as a prize, and she wasn't about to let me go off with just anyone." Her mother wouldn't let her go steady, and she was always encouraged to have more than one boyfriend at a time. If her mother didn't approve, she'd dismiss the boy, saying, "That's just puppy love. True love comes after marriage."

Keeping to her mother's rule of dating more than one man, Joanne had a boyfriend named Bill and a sexy South American boyfriend named Eduardo. Her mother favored Bill, because he was good husband material: the son of a wealthy, prominent family in the community and a law student. "This is what Daddy would have wanted for you," she told Joanne.

Joanne went through a series of breakups with both Bill and Eduardo, trying to please her mother one minute and trust her own feelings the next. She was actually more attracted to Eduardo, because he made her feel more like a woman than a girl. When he surprised Joanne and asked her to marry him, she accepted, but her mother went ballistic. "You can't do this to me!" she shouted. "He'll take you out of the country, and I'm so close to you." Joanne tried to reassure her that Eduardo would keep them in the States, but her mother wouldn't listen.

To make sure her daughter made the right choice, her mother asked an aunt, a respected matriarch in the family, to talk some sense into Joanne, and the strategy worked. Her aunt quickly convinced her that Bill would make the better husband. Part of Joanne's decision to marry Bill was that he was respectful of her mother and would provide for her mother after her marriage. Marrying Eduardo felt too much like she was abandoning her mother. "I had to do what my mother wanted. She was a widow," she explained. But even as she was walking down the aisle, Joanne still thought of Eduardo, dreaming that they'd one day be together if things didn't work out with Bill.

About ten years into her marriage and three kids later, Joanne realized she wasn't happy, but decided to stay until her children were older. She blamed her mother for having pressured her to marry Bill, and she began to rebel. She started voicing more opinions and defending them. She would be sarcastic to her mother, who would get hurt by Joanne's new tough style of communicating and withdraw. Joanne had an affair with another man and fell madly in love as a way out of the marriage.

When Joanne did find the courage to leave Bill, she distanced herself from her mother as well. She encouraged her mother to move out of state and eventually moved away herself. Once she moved to California, she continued to break from tradition and redesign her life, choosing new work, pursuing her own spirituality. She began to get closer to both her mother and children, who were now grown-up, but this time it was on her terms, not theirs.

At no time did Joanne totally cut off her relationship with her mother, but she did put a lot of distance between herself and her mother, partly to create safety and space for the life changes she was experiencing, and partly because she needed to create a new relationship with her. The old relationship of stuffing her feelings and doing what her mother wanted no longer worked for her.

As a teenager she told her mother what she wanted to hear, because this was easier than arguing with her about the issues. But as a woman, she found she had to be honest with her mother. She learned to ignore her mother's meddling comments and not buy into her "guilt schtick," as she called it. She shifted the emphasis to having fun with her mother and found that their relationship began to improve and lighten up.

Over a twenty-year period her relationship evolved to the point where she could be more like herself around her mother. She found her voice late in life and was finally able to confront her mother, even disagree with her, and handle the consequences. When she confronted her mother about Eduardo, her mother refused to believe that he had been that important in Joanne's life, but later apologized to her daughter for interfering in her choice of husband.

Refining Your Movements

When I heard Joanne's story, I was reminded of a visiting sensei's comments about *refining our movements*. She said that when we start our aikido practice, our movements are bigger, less focused, less powerful. Through years of practice our movements become smaller, more refined, almost imperceptible, but more powerful.

Joanne's first efforts to stand up to her mother were just like that. She was sarcastic, aggressive, going for shock value. It was as if she didn't believe she really had the power to take her life back, so she went overboard trying to prove it to her mother. But over the years, her efforts to create a new relationship became more refined, and she finally got what she wanted, the connection with minimal grief from her mother.

Like Joanne, if you stay in the game of pursuing what you want with your mother long enough, you will expend less effort in the drama and begin to sense your way more with your intuition. Your subtle, more focused actions will bring you greater rewards in the relationship.

How Bias Filters Affect Your Perception

What Joanne was describing as her mother's life experiences, those experiences that colored her advice to her daughter, are known as *bias filters*. Simply put, bias filters are feelings, life experiences, and preferences that affect our perception, the way we look at everything, see and hear other people, and make decisions. Joanne's mother was advising her through the bias filters of losing her husband, of minimizing her own sexuality, and wanting her daughter to be financially and emotionally secure in marriage. She had good intentions for her daughter, but her biases were definitely pushing her daughter's guilt buttons.

All mothers parent and advise through their bias filters, and push our guilt buttons with their preferences. And we do it, too, with our own biases that get in the way of our relationship with our mother. We can't change this about each other, but we do need to be aware of these biases and their ability to trigger our guilt. We need to be able to hear the biases in our mother's comments, and still find our own voice, which tells us to slow down and not overreact to her words.

Because our mother was our primary love object and taught us good from bad, we may be continuing to use her as a reference for everything we do in our lives. By doing this, we are at our mother's mercy, since we are making her the judge of right and wrong, and guilt cannot exist without a sense of wrongdoing.

It's important to note, though, that guilt is so toxic, no actual wrongdoing actually has to occur. Once our mothers hook us with an emotion, we can just perceive we've done something wrong or let her down, and we feel guilty. *Perceive* is the key word here, because the guilt we feel is directly tied to how we think we failed, not how we actually failed or didn't fail. It is the story we tell ourselves about what happened versus what actually happened.

One day, during my rebellious teenage years, I was mouthing off to my mother and she had it with me. She never hit us, but this time, she raised her hand to slap me. When she came near my face, I ducked and she hit her hand on the wall and broke it. I felt so terrible, so guilty. It scared me so much that I could hurt her like that, that from that moment on, I never had any problems with my mother, and today we're very close. She hardly ever thinks of this incident, but I never forgot it. It changed the whole tone of our relationship.   —Rhonda

Rhonda actually made her guilt worse by telling herself she was a bad daughter for hurting her mother, who actually had forgiven her long ago and hardly even remembered the incident. It was her perception of the incident, not her mother's, that kept fueling the guilt. Rhonda told me that she's never had a major disagreement with her mother since this incident, and I wondered if she wasn't somehow punishing herself by trying too hard to be the good, compliant daughter, but she assured me this was not the case. She said it did scare her into realizing that her relationship needed changing, that nothing was worth one or both of them getting hurt. That's when she decided to build a friendship with her mother, and they are still close today.

You may be doing the same thing, feeling guilty about something you did, that you're sure your mother is still upset about, only to find that she has long since forgotten the episode. If that is the case and you have made up your guilt, you need to unmake it by fine-tuning your story until you can let it go. You must see the situation for what it was, accept your part in it, and if you feel you've done something wrong, quickly forgive yourself, and aim toward more positive behavior in the future.

The most effective way to do this is to use *code expressions* of ten words or less to blast through all the shame. Code expressions are short phrases which cut through your mind chatter, where you spin the guilt stories, and give you the ability to move on.

TRY THIS

- The next time you feel like punishing yourself for something you've done, say out loud, "Silly me," and quickly follow it with "From now on I'll _____," and state the new behavior you want to do in the future.

This technique is so effective because it immediately dismisses the mistake and stops the guilt trip. It allows you to quickly forgive yourself and move on to more positive behavior.

If you can't quickly dismiss your mistakes and move on, you may find yourself using guilt to punish yourself even more. This punishment takes on several forms—you may replay the incident in your mind and relive the emotions and guilt; you may stay angry at yourself or your mother; you may sink into depression, convincing yourself that you deserve to feel bad because you've done something so terrible.

Sometimes you may actually want to be punished because it relieves you of your sense of wrongdoing. Bonnie found this to be true with her mother, as she was begging for punishment to absolve her of her guilt.

When I was in the sixth grade, I won the science fair with a project on the dangers of smoking cigarettes. That day on the bus home, some kids talked me into taking the pack of cigarettes I'd used in the experiment and going off campus to smoke them. I know, it wasn't the brightest idea, and to make matters worse, we got caught.

I was so embarrassed by my mistake, that I begged my mother to spank me as a punishment. It was the only thing that was going to make me feel better after such a stupid move. But she wouldn't do it. Instead, she gave me the ultimate guilt trip by looking sad and saying, "I'm just so hurt, I can't do it." It was much worse than getting spanked.   —Bonnie

When you learn to use the "Silly me . . . From now on" technique on a regular basis, you avoid the need to punish yourself or have others punish you, because it will stop the guilt trip (and punishment) before it even starts. It's another example of staying close to the moment, to what's happening right now, by forgiving yourself right when you've made the mistake, instead of letting the mistake wear on you and turn into full-blown drama.

Cultivating Mindful Awareness

If guilt is a learned response to failed expectations and the emotional hooks, then you can unlearn it by improving your perception and developing your ability to focus on what's really happening instead of what you think is happening.

Sometimes it's helpful to ask a few basic questions to tune into the situation. "What does my mother really want here?" "What do I want?" "How can we find common ground?" You don't need to overanalyze the situation—just ask a few simple questions to shift the faulty perception.

In the martial arts we are taught to give *mindful* awareness to our opponents, to stay connected to them and know where they are at all times. This mindful awareness is a relaxed alertness that allows us to sense our partners' movements. Aikido achieves this relaxed alertness by focusing our breath and attention on certain techniques. It becomes clear real soon if we have faulty perceptions of where they are moving, because we will lose our connection with them and put ourselves in harm's way.

To practice mindful awareness, you must develop a quieting practice away from your mother that will prepare you to be more alert when you are in her presence. There are a number of ways to do this. Some women use prayer or meditation to quiet themselves; others walk on the beach or simply stare into a beautiful fire. There are many tapes available which provide quiet sounds, such as the trickling of a waterfall, which will lull your mind into stillness and allow creativity and insight to come in.

TRY THIS

- Set your watch or timer for fifteen minutes.
- Sit comfortably in a chair and close your eyes.
- Take ten deep breaths and let your breathing relax to a more normal place.
- Imagine your mind as a blank screen and, each time you get a thought, allow the picture to come on the screen and gently scroll off to the side.

Sometimes your thoughts will look like pictures—other times, they'll look like sound waves or seem like feelings. Whatever their form, allow them to come in and scroll off the screen.

- Allow your mind to become the blank screen.
- When the alarm sounds, wake up and resume your normal activity.

The more you practice quieting your mind, the more you'll be able to carry your mental alertness into all your interactions with your mother. When you are mindfully aware of where you're moving with your mother, you are less likely to be hooked into one of her guilt trips, because you are more accurately perceiving where she is going with her comments and you are staying close to the emotion without getting sucked into the drama. You are more flexible, because you are less attached to things happening a certain way.

Expecting Mother's Emotional Hooks

Jewish mother and comedienne Mary Jo Steiner tells her audiences, "At my bank they just installed a Jewish mother ATM machine. Before it gives you any money, a voice says, 'So, what did you do with the last $20 I gave you?' "

Who needs these ATMs when your mother is the best-talking guilt machine around? If there is anything you can count on, it's your mother throwing you an emotional hook, a look, a one-liner to get things rolling. I remember watching a television show where a mother kept repeating, "Oh, that's all right." Four little words, but she had total control of her daughter with her looks and whining tone.

A friend of mine shared that whenever she'd express an idea her mother didn't approve of, her mother would look at her as if she was as dumb as a fence post and say, "Who told you that?" Translation: just what makes you think you have an original thought anyway? Again, four little words, and she was off and running with her mother.

My mother's personal favorite was "Wait till you grow up—I hope you have a daughter just like you." I call it her Bulgarian curse, because I did have two daughters, and they are just like her and me, intense in every way.

SOME OF ERMA BOMBECK'S FAVORITE "GUILT GRABBERS"

- I'm going to send all that food you left on your plate to all the starving children in Armenia.
- Do you want Mommy to leave the house and never come back?
- You're going to drive me to an early grave.
- That's what you get for not listening.
- I'm only one person.

from *Motherhood: The Second Oldest Profession*

Once you understand that it can take your mother less than ten seconds to hook you, you can at least be prepared to receive some zingers. This is one case where expecting the worst just might pay off. If your mother is in the habit of hooking you, and you expect these kinds of comments and moves from her, you won't be surprised and may actually be able to laugh at some of them. You can try other techniques such as wearing dark sunglasses all the time so she can't see your eyes and know if she's getting to you, but she'll probably think you have a drug problem and call Narcotics Anonymous.

Just because your mother throws you a hook, doesn't mean you have to bite. It's what you do with it that counts. You can ignore it, laugh at it, interrupt it, deflect it, argue with it—the choice is yours. Layering a funny picture on top of whatever your mother is saying can help you keep your sense of humor and sidestep the guilt.

IMAGINE THIS

Imagine you are a judge at the Guilt Olympics and your mother is going for the gold against all the other mothers. Every time she throws out a zinger, mentally hold up a scorecard and think, "That's an 8.2 or 9.1!" or "Oooh! That's a perfect 10!" Get the picture? It's hard to stay mad at your mother when you're rating her best shots at you.

The worst thing you can do is react to it by defending yourself, explaining too much about the situation or your decision, or just plain arguing with her. This will only escalate the problem between you, and give your mother more material to churn in the process. No matter how much she hooks you, this isn't the time to break into a rousing rendition of "Feelings" and bare your soul. You need to stay cool and regroup for a more positive response. You need to listen to your own voice and not overreact to her words.

You and Your Mother Are Cocreators of an Outcome

Two authors, C. Richard Pohl and Bob Gardenhire III, wrote an article for *Aikido Magazine* in which they spoke about an *awareness of interwovenness,* of cocreating an outcome with another person:

> Eventually, one discovers that other people are not the only "enemies" or the only sources of disturbance in one's life. When people interact, the question always is "What are we doing together?" When something goes well, people make it happen together. When something does not go well, people make that happen together.
>
> Up to this point, we still think in categories of opposition—friend vs. enemy, etc. At the point where interwovenness fully dawns, however, blaming, categorizing, and dismissing dissolve. None can escape responsibility since it is clear that we are cocreators of an outcome.

This concept of cocreating an outcome has several applications in your dealings with your mother. It's not your mother against you or you against your mother, but you and your mother in this together. Guilt can't take place without both players. If you've created conflict together, you can also create peace together. It just requires more consciousness and perseverance.

What I'm asking you to do here is shift from victim thinking—from what she's doing to you to what you're doing to each other. Once either one of you (the person with the higher insight) realizes this, you can try something new and create a different outcome.

I recently met a woman who was complaining about the terrible relationship she had with her mother, that they hadn't spoken for months. She was blaming the problems on a stepfather who had come between them and, in her opinion, was keeping her away from her mother. She kept insisting that her mother be the one to make the first move toward reconciliation because she was the mother and should know better. I asked this woman to make the first move herself, to define her own relationship with her mother instead of letting others define it for her. She listened, but had tremendous resistance to taking action to change things. She failed to see how she was cocreating a poor relationship with her mother. It was easier for her to keep blaming her stepfather.

As Pohl and Gardenhire point out, blame drops away when you realize you're in this outcome together. You have to let go of your right-and-wrong thinking and go to higher ground. When you change your part in the dynamic between you and your mother, you create a different outcome, for you at least, and feel better in the process. This doesn't mean you change your mother, but you change your behavior around your mother and the way you feel when you're around her. The result is you have a sense of being more in control of your life instead of feeling at your mother's mercy.

For example, your mother may have a habit of calling you in the evening and dumping her problems on you just as you're trying to unwind from work. It's dinnertime, the witching hour for your kids, and to make matters worst, your husband comes home and is upset that you're on the phone again with your mother. He remembers the last time you talked, and he doesn't feel like playing therapist that evening. When you try to get off the phone, your mother throws out an emotional hook, "You're always too busy to talk to me." Just then you realize you've burned dinner and your family's starving.

You may think there's nothing you can do about this problem, that you have to talk to your mother, no matter when she calls. You think you're being the good daughter, available at your mother's beck and call, but you're alienating your own family in the process. And if you're really honest with yourself, you'd admit that you don't enjoy these calls with your mother because you're too stressed out.

If you don't believe you're cocreating the problem, you're fooling yourself. The remedy for this is asking yourself what you want (to come home and unwind after work and enjoy your family). Then you need to make a decision not to answer calls between 5:00 and 8:00 P.M., and instead make a time to call your mother when it best fits into your schedule. How will your mother react? You don't exactly know. She may try to blame you for not being there for her. She may get angry and not call for a few days or weeks. Or she may decide to let go and enjoy the times you do call.

The point is, it doesn't matter how she reacts—you still feel in control and are happier with your decision because it fits your life. You have time to decompress from the day, help the kids with homework or read them a book, and greet your husband with a smile instead of the stress mask you usually show him. Dinnertime is now a relaxed, nurturing time for you and your family.

Changing your part has allowed you to change the outcome with your mother. You are committed to keeping a connection with her, but doing it on your terms, so you can enjoy it more. Chances are your mother will enjoy it more, too, as you will be more relaxed and emotionally present when you do talk to her.

How to Disagree with Your Mother and Handle the Emotional Fallout

There's a difference between staying in control of your life and trying to control other people or circumstances. Staying in control is making those decisions, taking those actions that make you feel calm inside. Trying to control others is becoming overinvolved in their lives, telling them what to do, manipulating their behavior to fit your needs.

LOCUS OF CONTROL

Because guilt makes you feel out of control, you may waste time trying to control people or things out of your center of influence. Locus of control is that center of things (namely your thoughts, decisions, actions) that you have control over. Everything else, including your mother's reactions, is out of your control.

Disagreeing with your mother can make you feel out of control because you fear that you will lose her love or approval. You don't know how your mother will react and just thinking about this can be like facing the giant black hole of the universe. You're so afraid to take the risk, but at the same time so frustrated with yourself that you can't hold your own around your mother. To bridge that fear gap you must be simultaneously committed to staying connected to your mother and staying in control of your life by making decisions and taking actions that empower you.

TRY THIS

What if, in the phone example mentioned earlier, your mother would have told you, "You only talk to me when it fits into your schedule." This could hook you into a guilt trip for sure, but you still have some choices about how you want to respond:

- You can buy into it and feel bad and go back to your old pattern of letting your mother call anytime, but soon you'll be angry with yourself because you let your mother bully you into a self-defeating move.
- You can start to explain yourself and give your mother more material to attack or criticize.
- You can listen, say as little as possible, reduce your responses to mere "uh-huhs" and say, "I understand, and this is what works for me."

The effectiveness of the *"I understand, and this is what works for me"* technique is based on three things:

1. using the word "and" instead of "but" because "but" sets up more conflict;
2. repeating the phrase, because if your mother's arguing with you, she's out of control herself and this code expression will interrupt her verbal pattern;
3. being consistent—maintaining a connection with her, but sticking to your position.

The beauty of using the "I understand and this is what works for me" phrase is you are giving your mother feedback that you hear her side of things while still bringing her back to your decision. This posture is still caring for your mother (you want to talk to her on the phone, have a relationship with her), but you are not being too nice at your own expense. And while you are disagreeing with her, you aren't falling into the trap of explaining yourself too much. This would send the wrong message to yourself that you are a nobody and can only justify your decisions with a lot of words.

You are somebody in our own right and do not have to explain or rationalize your decisions to your mother. The old adage "fake it till you make it" is especially apropos here, since it's better to fake confidence until it becomes a habit for you. Lack of confidence in yourself merely gives your mother more openings to run guilt trips on you.

What will your mother do? She may protest further and act out, but eventually, all things, even your mother, will bend to a constant. What choice does she have if she wants to stay in a relationship with you?

Ellen's Story: Having the Courage to Disagree with Her Mother

When I interviewed Ellen she told me how scary it finally was to disagree with her mother. "I had been raised to never use the 'f' ('father') word around my mother. Dad was like this phantom—nothing was ever said about him; there were never any pictures of him. Any time I'd mention him, my mother would get angry." Ellen learned to stop asking. But when she was thirty years old, she decided, against her mother's advice, to take action to find her father. "I realized I needed to do something for me, even though my mother had said no," she told me.

At first, Ellen wanted her mother to approve of her decision, to join her in the search. "I had this all figured out, that if she met or dealt with my father, then she'd feel better about the past." But this just caused more problems between her and her mother, because her mother had no intention of facing Ellen's father. Consumed with her own emotions, her mother became very angry at Ellen and pulled away from her daughter.

At one point, Ellen's mother told her, "Don't call me Mother anymore," a hook if there ever was one, and stopped answering Ellen's calls. But Ellen made a decision to stay connected to her mother, to leave messages on her machine and ask other family members about her. One time she left presents for her mother and was hurt to find them returned unopened on her doorstep.

She had no indication from her mother's words or actions that they would ever have a relationship again. "It was like my mother and I were going from Point A to Point B, and it was a hell of a scary ride," she told me. "At times I didn't think Point B existed."

Ellen continued to call her mother every week, and if her mother did talk to her, they'd fight. Things didn't look very hopeful for their relationship, until one Sunday, when Ellen saw her mother at church and followed her intuition to invite her to dinner. To her surprise, her mother accepted, and this opened the door for a reconciliation.

Her mother was still angry about Ellen's decision to find her father, but she decided to drop it. And Ellen decided to drop her agenda, to let her mother come (or not come) to her own healing, whatever was best for her.

Ellen did find her father and had dinner with him and realized that after all these years, he still wasn't interested in being an active part of her life. It made her appreciate her mother even more. And once she realized he was married to someone else when her mother became pregnant with her, she understood her mother's need never to face him again.

It was painful for Ellen to disagree with her mother, but she did grow from the experience. She learned how important it was to stick to her own decision and to bring her mother back to that decision if necessary. She learned to make decisions for herself and not have any other hidden agendas for her mother. And she learned how to allow her mother to have her own reactions to and choices about her decision.

Because Ellen was equally committed to following through on her decision and to staying in a relationship with her mother, she was able to hold the space for her mother to eventually come around. Her mother did yield to Ellen's decision, not because she planned to become part of it, but because she saw Ellen was not going to change her mind. And Ellen faced her worst fear, losing her mother's love and approval, yet regained them both when she held firm to her decision.

Ellen's advice to other women is: "Stay connected to your mother, no matter what, because it's a process, everyone's growing, and when the healing's there, you can't be on vacation. It isn't a death sentence when things don't work. Hang in there."

How has hanging in there paid off for Ellen? She has great relationships with both her mother and her daughter and has recently become engaged to a wonderful man who shares in this deep connection with her family. "My girlfriends all knew my mother very well when I was growing up, and they knew so much about our relationship. They're surprised we healed this. They say that whenever they feel hopeless in their relationships, they think of us, that we're a real inspiration to them."

Guilt Is the Gift That Keeps on Giving

When I told my friend Mary Jo I was writing about guilt, she said, "You're writing about mothers. The whole book is about guilt." Are the words mother and guilt that synonymous? We might think so, judging from the amount of time we spend wallowing in it.

Guilt is destructive. Guilt is wasted energy. Guilt keeps us from the relationship we want by making us feel worse about ourselves. Guilt is the gift that keeps on giving. If it's not our mothers giving it to us, it's us giving it to ourselves with that voice in our head that we like to call our mother's anyway.

There comes a point in our journey as mothers and daughters when we have to scream, "Enough already," and quiet the guilt demons once and for all. We have to learn how to let go of our impossible expectations of each other, how to sidestep the hooks, how to love more and blame less, how to disagree and still stay in the relationship.

When we learn these things, guilt will no longer have the power over us that it's held in the past, and we, too, can have relationships that will inspire others.

TWO

The Never-Good-Enough Blues:

Handling Your Mother's Criticism

The last time I was looking for a job, I received three

rejection letters: two from businesses and

one from my mother.

Just When You Think You're Managing Your Life Well

You think you're giving your mother a nice gift, and your mother says, "I know how much these barbecues cost. Why did you get me the small one?"

You think you're eating a healthy breakfast of yogurt and granola, and your mother says, "I'd rather die ten years sooner than eat that bird food you eat."

You think you're driving off in the car of your dreams, and your mother says, "Funny, I thought a Mercedes would be more luxurious inside. Why didn't you just buy a Lincoln Town Car?"

You think you're going to wow your classmates at the class reunion with your gorgeous low-cut dress, and your mother says, "That dress was made for a woman with a real bust. You better buy a Miracle bra."

You think you're going on a safe vacation, and your mother says, "I wouldn't travel to that part of the world. It's filled with terrorists!"

You think your husband is making great progress with his career, and your mother says, "Hasn't that husband of yours been promoted to manager yet?"

You think you're doing a wonderful job raising your daughter, and your mother says, "I never let you do that when you were a child. Who's in charge here?"

You think you're being a compassionate pet owner by letting your golden retriever stay inside, and your mother says, "How can you stand living on top of this much hair?"

If only we could live with our mothers' criticism, learn to laugh at it. But as this repartee illustrates, our critical mothers invade every area of our lives: our personal appearance, our house, our husband, our children, even the darn dog! And they don't stop there—they criticize our jobs, our decisions, our capabilities so much that we doubt ourselves.

Donna Marie told me her mother would read the labels on her makeup and criticize her for spending too much money. "To this day, I take the labels off of everything I buy," she said. "It'll be a real growth experience for me to leave the labels on someday." Funny how we can anchor into our mothers' criticism in the most unusual ways, and form our habits and behaviors around it.

When our mothers criticize us to this degree, they are often clueless about the impact their criticism has on us. They may think they're just being direct or honest, when we feel they're being rude and insensitive. They may think they are protecting us, when we feel they're trying to tell us what to do.

Living with this criticism can leave us feeling like we'll never be good enough for our mothers and drive us to extremes: becoming perfectionists or superstars just to prove them wrong or ruining our lives because we never think we'll please them anyway. On one end of the spectrum, we graduate with honors, set national sales records, become model mothers ourselves or CEOs of major corporations. On the other end, we screw up our own lives so badly with addictions to men, shopping, food, alcohol, or drugs, we can't possibly please our mothers—then at least we are off the hook.

We may actually find such failure comforting, because we can continue to blame our mothers for ruining our lives. It can be more difficult living outside our mothers' criticism, because it means we have to take responsibility for our own actions and emotional well-being.

Donna Marie told me her mother was so picky, she would notice the one thing wrong, instead of the nine things right out of every ten things done. She was so afraid Donna Marie would make a mistake at her dance recital, she stayed behind the curtain and whispered the dance steps from the wings. "It was so impossible to please her, I developed an attitude that unless I could do something absolutely perfectly, why even bother to try," Donna Marie confided.

Another woman told me that her mother was so critical of her in the kitchen, she couldn't even boil water around her. For years she avoided cooking, doing the bare minimum, until she realized her mother's criticism and anger had affected her relationship with food. After her mother's death, she rediscovered a love of cooking as a way to express her creativity and nurture herself.

DRAMA TRAP: BECOMING HELPLESS AROUND YOUR MOTHER'S CRITICISM

If you have an overly critical mother, the worst danger is buying into that criticism and doubting your own worth and capabilities. You can become so unsure of yourself that you can't complete even the simplest tasks around your mother.

This learned helplessness around our mothers can seriously impact our lives, the way we approach our relationships and careers, because it runs deep into our subconscious to the core of who we are. The best remedy to break free of this helplessness is acting confidently on our own behalf, because it retrains our subconscious into new beliefs, which can give our self-esteem a much-needed boost.

The daughter who reignited her love of cooking did just that. She took cooking courses, invited friends over for dinner, cooked special meals for herself. With each action, she formed a new belief that she loved cooking and was capable in the kitchen. And this new confidence in the kitchen made her feel like a more capable person in general.

How to Stop Feeding the Critic

The problem is we give our critical mothers too much material to criticize. We have juicy visits or long conversations on the phone with them, telling them every intimate detail of our lives, and then wonder why they take so many shots at us.

Some mothers actually feed on this desire to tell everything, by saying it is a sign of closeness between them and their daughters. But the truth is sharing too much information can get us enmeshed in each other's lives in an unhealthy way by placing too much of an emotional burden on each other. It puts mothers in a position where they are more likely to interfere with their daughters' decisions, because they know too much, and daughters in a position where they are likely to ask too much advice of their mothers, instead of acting independently and learning from their own mistakes.

Telling too much can actually be an anxiety reaction, in which we are so nervous around our mothers that we begin talking obsessively to fill the void of our uncomfortableness. The brain can only handle about three to seven pieces of information at the same time, yet most of us try to scan fifteen to twenty items and wonder why we suffer from brain fog. When we do that, our brain goes into overload and we can actually forget what we said or did, because we were that stressed out. If you think you've been going brain-dead around your mother, this may be the reason for it.

TRY THIS

One of the best ways to turn your relationship around with your critical mother is to keep the conversation short and upbeat. The next time you talk to her on the phone try this:

• Announce your departure up front.

Tell her that you only have 5 minutes to talk, because you're on your way out, but you wanted to touch base with her (remember, don't give too much information or explanation).

• Set a kitchen timer for 5 minutes.
• Give her the flash report, the short upbeat news since you last talked. Keep this to 1–2 minutes.
• Ask her what's new and give her 1–2 minutes to talk. Just listen.
• Remind her you're leaving and end with a short phrase like: "Love you, Mother" or "Talk to you soon."

If your mother starts to criticize you, let it go, and redirect the conversation to a new topic. Longer conversations can be reserved for visits in person or planned in advance by writing some brief notes before calling your mother.

By having shorter, more upbeat conversations, you create less opportunity for your mother to criticize you. Too often you get trapped on the phone, defending your position or trying to prove your mother wrong at the expense of your relationship. You must ask yourself, "Do I want to be right or do I want to have a relationship with my mother?" If you want to have a relationship with your mother, do what works.

Once you create more positive communication, you will actually enjoy each other more, because your time together won't be so problem-laden or crisis-driven. You may even think your mother is being less critical, when, in fact, she's responding to your taking responsibility for your communication to her. You can't change her reactions, but you can change what you decide to tell her, and that can change the whole tone of your relationship.

RELATIONSHIPS ARE FOR SHARING

Relationships are for sharing and the quality of what you share is the quality of the relationship. If you share the problems, the grief, the drama, your relationship will be all those things. If, on the other hand, you share the joy, the love, the laughter, your relationship will reflect those qualities instead.

A friend of mine was going home for a visit with her mother and wanted some last-minute advice about how she could have a better time with her. I asked her, "What do you want?" She looked at me with a blank look on her face, and said, "I don't know. I never allowed myself to think about it, because I didn't think I could get what I wanted."

She explained that her mother is very critical of her life and values, that it isn't safe for her to share intimate details with her, because her mother talks to her other sisters and brothers about her. She expressed sadness that, as the middle child in a large family, she never really felt the love and nurturing she wanted from her mother. She felt her mother was too self-absorbed and that she'd have to read up about "narcissism complex" (a psychological term that refers to people who have excessive admiration of themselves which affects their ability to love and nurture others) before the visit.

DRAMA TRAP: CLASSIFYING YOUR MOTHER ACCORDING TO PSYCHOLOGICAL STEREOTYPES

What if I told you that your mother was a "paranoid schizophrenic"? Would this mean anything to you? Would you know how to deal with her on a daily basis?

If you treat your mother like a case study, she'll pick up on this and dismiss your psychobabble in an instant. Unless your mother needs to be institutionalized, which is rarely the case, just call her difficult or impossible and accept the fact that whatever she is, she's yours, and find some ways to get along with her.

I told my friend to forget "narcissism complex" and just keep asking herself what she wanted in her relationship with her mother. I asked her what worked during their last visit, and she said they enjoyed shopping together, that it was fun and easy to be together. I encouraged her to do that again and find other areas of common ground where she and her mother could enjoy quality time together. I also encouraged her to let her mother keep to her own routine as much as possible, and suggested that she join in where she could.

My friend tried my advice and actually had one of the best visits she's ever had with her mother. She went to the gym with her, and while her mother was swimming laps, she took an aerobics class. After class, her mother introduced her friends to her daughter and they all swooned over her grandchild, which made my friend feel great. Both she and her mother came home from the gym feeling that they'd shared a great time together, and my friend felt more loved and nurtured in the relationship. She didn't have to analyze or confront her mother or even discuss boundaries. She didn't need to read up on the narcissism complex. She just needed to find common ground and share a good time with her mother, which set her on the course of having both a better visit and a better relationship with her mother.

If you're wondering why this is so simple, it's because it is. We are the ones who have made our relationships so complicated, and it doesn't have to be this way. When we practice sharing good times—and we do this often enough that it becomes habit—we open ourselves to feeling the love and nurturing we've always wanted, and in some ways, the relationship takes care of itself. It becomes the by-product of the care and attention we practice with each other.

Understanding Critical Distance in Our Relationship with Mother

To create the relationships we want, there must be an element of trust and safety in our dealings with each other, a balance between our connection and our separateness. A visiting sensei to our dojo (aikido facility/community) taught us about *critical distance*, a term used in the sport of Western fencing which has applications to both aikido practice and our relationships with our mothers. He showed us how being too close to our partners was actually life-threatening in the martial sense, that we must stand back far enough to be connected, engage in combat if needed, but also maintain some distance to defend ourselves.

In our relationship with our mother, we must be separate enough to distance ourselves from the criticism, but connected enough to be able to move toward the relationship we want. When we experience our mothers' criticism, it can erode any foundation of trust that might have already been there and make us want to withdraw even more. Yet we must balance this desire with the desire to draw close and share true intimacy with our mothers.

CRITICAL DISTANCE

Critical distance is that emotional space between you and your mother which allows you to take care of yourself and still stay in a relationship with her. It provides safety for both of you.

If we are engaging in ongoing dramas of fighting, separating, and coming back together, we haven't found the critical distance in our relationship. We find it by leaning into our own intuition more, noticing which actions take us closer to our mothers and which ones create conflict, noticing what feels comfortable for us and what makes us want to back up. This distance will be different for every mother and daughter.

My friend was getting a sense of her own critical distance with her
mother before she went home on her visit. Part of the reason she didn't
feel safe was she was going to be in closer physical and emotional prox-
imity to her impossible mother. In some ways it had been easier to
deal with her when she was three thousand miles away. Now she was
going back into her mother's environment, her power base.

She also didn't feel safe going home, because her mother couldn't be
trusted to keep information confidential, and she was afraid that in
their sharing, she might reveal something so personal about herself
that her mother would turn and tell her brothers and sisters. Her past
experience with her mother had taught her to be careful in this area
and rightfully so. All the more reason she should limit what information
she'd give her mother during their time together.

The point is: none of these fears kept my friend from enjoying a
good visit with her mother because she was able to create the safety and
intimacy she needed to experience quality time with her. She had found
the balance, the critical distance in her relationship that allowed her to
take care of herself and stay in a relationship with her mother.

How to Separate Mother
from Her Internal Critic:

Not only do we need to separate our life from our mother's life, but we
also need to separate our mother from her internal critic. As children
we are helpless to hear her pain in the words she hurls at us . . . that re-
alization comes much later in our lives, if we're lucky. But when we do
hear it, we are free to feel compassion for our mother and can finally
let go of all the pain we've been holding in our childhood memories.

Many of us daughters still miss this connection between our mother's
dissatisfaction with herself and her need to criticize us. We mistakenly
think she doesn't care, that she's somehow evil and out to get us. We be-

lieved in childhood that everything was about us, and we desperately cling to that belief for our own survival. Ironically, it is this belief that trips us up the most, because it puts our happiness, the relationship we truly want with our mother, out of our reach.

Sometimes it takes being mothers ourselves to see our mother as a separate woman behind the words. It's humbling to open our mouths and hear our mother's words criticizing our own children. We quickly realize that it is we who are hurting the most and that criticizing our children won't help. One day it finally dawns on us that our mother probably had her own reasons and motivations for yelling at us, too, that it actually had more to do with her frustrations and dissatisfaction with herself than with us. In fact, if we're really honest with ourselves, we'll marvel at how well our mother did given her life circumstances.

In order for you to separate your mother from her critic, you must first shift your beliefs about her and understand who she really is.

NEW BELIEFS ABOUT YOUR MOTHER

- Your mother and you share the same dream: what's best for you.
- Your mother is not evil . . . she is not out to hurt you or get you.
- Your mother is doing the best she can with the options she sees for herself.
- Your mother's criticism is a failed attempt to communicate her love and concern for you.
- Your mother's criticism is more about her than you.
- Your mother's criticism is masking other motivations.

Let's play devil's advocate and challenge these beliefs. Why? Because just reading these beliefs, you've probably challenged them already:

WHAT'S BEST FOR ME—ARE YOU KIDDING?

In the heat of your mother's criticism, you may not believe this, but it is actually her desire for "the good life" for you that keep the barbs coming. What is the good life?—whatever your mother wanted and didn't get, anything better than the life your mother's currently living. The more unhappy your mother is, the more she wants a better life for you. You must remember her wanting this for you doesn't mean she actually knows how to get it for you, but it can help explain why she puts the heat on you or your spouse.

NOT EVIL OR OUT TO HURT ME?—YOU HAVEN'T MET MY MOTHER.

Your mother's comments and actions can seem so cruel that you're tempted to believe she has a plan to ruin your life. Your mother has a plan all right, called "the good life," and she is determined to force-feed this to you sometimes at your own expense. That's why she can be so demanding about your life, your education, your choice of a husband. Your mother may not know when to stop, when to turn it off, so she could become overinvolved in your life. But at no time is the underlying feeling she has for you bad or evil, no matter how poorly she behaves.

What about those mothers who abuse or murder their children? How can we say they didn't want to hurt their children? Erma Bombeck mentions such a woman in the introduction of *Motherhood: The Second Oldest Profession.* "Judy was incarcerated in a Southern prison for the unspeakable crime of killing her child. . . . She passed time in solitary confinement reading some of my earlier books. After she read and reread some of them, she wrote to me, 'Had I known mothers could laugh at those things, I probably wouldn't be where I am today.' " We can hear the tone of repentance in this woman's words, her underlying desire not to hurt her child.

To feel compassion for women who abuse their children, you must fully understand their mind-set, that at the time they hurt their children, they felt so trapped, they saw no other options for themselves. They were so out of control themselves, their act of violence was their last desperate act to regain control. Like Judy, they didn't know they could laugh at something or ask a friend to watch their child so they could take some time to regroup and see new options for themselves.

All they knew, all they felt at the time was, "I can't get through to my child. I can't make her stop crying (or whatever). Why is she doing this to me? What's it going to take for her to hear me?" All they wanted was to make the child stop the offending behavior, so they could feel in control of themselves again. Afterward, they might have felt remorse like Judy did, or maybe even so much pain they wanted to kill themselves, but at the time their act of violence seemed like the only thing they could do. When you understand their thinking, you can see that even these mothers are not evil—lost, but not evil.

And these mothers didn't get lost overnight. They often came from horrible backgrounds themselves or were in abusive relationships that made them feel even more out of control. They never felt the love themselves to extend to their own children.

Some women were raised by mothers who could be called abusive and violent, and they can't imagine how they will get past this to forgive their mothers and move on. But until they do, they are stuck being victims and can't fully pick up their lives or the relationships they want. I'm not suggesting glossing over the past, but rather taking the time to understand the abusive mother's pain and confusion through this new insight.

DOING THE BEST SHE CAN WITH THE OPTIONS SHE SEES FOR HERSELF—WHY CAN'T SHE DO WHAT I WANT HER TO DO?

Remember that your mother is from a different generation and you can't expect her to see things the way you do. Beth confided that she and her mother often clash about her need to have time to nurture herself. She tells her mother that sometimes her needs have to come first, that taking care of herself is the best way to take care of her family. But her mother still insists that this is a selfish attitude and that Beth should put her family first.

"Trying to explain this to her is 'almost a foreign language,'" Beth told me, and she's right—it is. In her mother's generation, taking time for solitude and for nurturing oneself was considered selfish and not encouraged by her husband or peers. Her mother simply doesn't see this as an option for her daughter or herself.

Our mothers' criticisms are often generated by these kinds of *blind spots,* those options they can't see for themselves or their daughter. By contrast, we daughters, conditioned by a different generation of choices, may see several options and can't understand why our mothers can see only one or two. We become frustrated with their old-fashioned thinking and want to make them wrong when conflict arises.

Your Mother's Criticism Is a Failed Attempt to Communicate Love and Concern for You—Why Can't My Mother Just Tell Me She Loves Me?

Your mother may not know how to tell you or show you how much she loves you. She simply may not be able to give you hugs and kisses, compliments, and encouragement. If this is the case, her criticism becomes a series of *communication misfires,* failed attempts at expressing her love and concern for you.

The challenge of living with such a mother is you either tune her out altogether or you hear everything she says as criticism. You may start to buy into her emotional aloofness and believe she's incapable of giving you the love and nurturing you want.

You have to understand that expressing feelings is a relatively new luxury you and I may have enjoyed, while people in your mother's generation were suspicious about such things. Back then people were considered weak if they expressed themselves—they were just supposed to handle their problems. Your mother may have been raised herself by a mother who couldn't express her feelings or one who smothered her with affection, and this may be why she is the way she is.

Your job is not to analyze your mother, but to keep treating her with the same love and affection you want from her. When you create the space for intimacy, she just may surprise you and step into that space with her own feelings.

YOUR MOTHER'S CRITICISM IS MORE ABOUT HER THAN YOU—SO DON'T TAKE IT PERSONALLY.

Don't take it personally? This woman's telling me how to run my life, and I shouldn't take it personally? No, you shouldn't. Your mother is the most complex mammal on the planet, and by now you should be getting a clue that it is not what she says, but the *subtext* that counts. (*Subtex* is the underlying thoughts, emotions, or story behind your mother's words.)

One woman was complaining to me that her mother was always nagging her about painting her house. She was upset that her mother didn't understand how tired she was after work, that painting was the last thing she wanted to do.

I listened to her a few minutes, and asked, "What do you think your mother really wants?" For a moment, she looked at me dumbfounded, then said, "I guess she wants me to live in a house that looks nice" (a.k.a. "the good life"), and I suggested that she probably wanted something else, to spend time with her daughter. Painting the house was just her mother's excuse (criticism) for nagging her daughter about what she really wanted.

I asked her if she and her mother had ever painted before, and she said yes. Then I asked her if she would be willing to let mother paint her house and join in for some of it. She started to laugh, and I could see her shoulders drop and her eyes twinkle as she thought about letting her mother paint the house. She told me her mother was retired, in great shape, and might actually enjoy it. In this case, going with the flow, giving her mother what she wanted, and joining in where she could, would be much easier than staying stuck in the same old battle.

YOUR MOTHER'S CRITICISM IS MASKING OTHER MOTIVATIONS.

Facing your mother's criticism is frustrating because you may not know or understand what's behind it. You simply can't make sense of her contradictory comments and actions. One minute she may be expressing her concern for you, and the next she may be competing with you. The important point here is to understand that *something else* is driving your mother, and it probably has nothing to do with you.

For example, a mother may get irritable when she drives her kids to dance lessons. Why?—she had to drop dance lessons when she was a kid because her mother and father told her they couldn't afford it. This may play out in the mother's life by her criticizing or nagging her daughter for not taking better care of her dance costume, or complaining about all the time dance lessons are taking away from the family. This mother's criticism of her daughter is masking her hurt feelings about having to drop dance or perhaps her desire to take dance herself.

Once you begin to understand these motivations behind your mother's criticism, you can begin to take your mother's criticism more lightly and sidestep much of your conflict with her. You realize you can't change her, but you can change the way you take the criticism, and this becomes the new stable base for your relationship.

CREATE A STABLE BASE

If you are feeling overwhelmed by your mother's criticism, stop and review these new beliefs about your mother. It will help you create a stable base from which to handle the emotion.

Handling the Underlying Motivations of Your Mother's Criticism

To get to the place where you can shake off most of your mother's criticism, you must first understand how to handle the underlying motivations behind her words. Some of the most common motivations are:

- Competition
- Overprotectiveness
- Emotional Neediness
- Control

COMPETITION

If your mother's motivation for criticizing you is competition, she is not feeling good about herself and is trying to win at your expense. Your life is her last shot at claiming lost youth or lost dreams, and she may hold you accountable to impossible standards that she herself wasn't able to keep. Criticizing you is her way of keeping you in the one-down position so she can feel good about herself. If you should happen to meet her impossible standards, she will change the rules of the game to keep the competition going.

Marilyn's mother—a beautiful, petite woman, used to a constant stream of male admiration—was criticizing Marilyn's weight out of an underlying motivation to compete with her. She couldn't stand to see her daughter grow up and become beautiful and sensual in her own right. Her message to Marilyn was "You're too big"—"such a big baby, you almost killed me" (talk about the ultimate guilt trip!), a "big girl," "big-boned," when the truth was Marilyn was thin enough to model for a local store. In this case her mother's impossible standard was asking Marilyn to be as petite as she was, when in fact Marilyn was taller and bigger than her mother and could never be that way.

Marilyn bought into this message so strongly that she hated her own body and thought she was too big to be beautiful. She wouldn't go out for cheerleading, because she thought she was too fat. She wouldn't accept a date with one boy because she didn't want him to see her in her bathing suit. And when she got engaged to be married, she decided she'd better sleep with her fiancé first—that way if he rejected her body, she would know if she should call off the wedding.

When Marilyn did become thin, as her mother wanted her to, she didn't find the approval she'd hoped for. Marilyn had been on a vacation with her mother and was receiving lots of attention and invitations from male admirers. When she told her mother how good this felt, her mother said, "They probably thought you were a hooker."

Marilyn was devastated. What was the point of all the criticism if now that she was thin and gorgeous, her mother didn't notice? Her mother noticed all right. She just changed the rules of the game to stay in the one-up position. It was her way of keeping her daughter in line, leveling the playing field for more competition.

If you feel competition is your mother's motivation for criticizing you, understand that you will never win playing your mother's game. Just when you think you have a leg up, she'll change the rules of the game on you. Instead, you must try some new strategies:

- Realize that your mother's standards may be impossible and set your own standards for your behavior.
- Don't announce every personal victory to your mother and expect her praise and approval.
- If you do tell your mother about your wins, try acknowledging her contribution to your victory, so she can feel it's her win, too.
- Learn to affirm yourself and celebrate your wins alone or with a special group of friends who will cheer you on.
- Support your mother in feeling good about herself by praising her for her accomplishments.
- Encourage your mother in doing the things she loves so she can feel like she's winning in her life.

OVERPROTECTIVENESS

If your mother's motivation for criticizing you is overprotectiveness, it could mean she wants you to play it safe and avoid some of the pain and hard knocks she experienced. When your mother is in this mode, she has a vivid picture of the good life she wants for you, and if you are not living up to that picture, she will be critical of you.

My mother often joked about going to the School of Hard Knocks, but inside it was no laughing matter. Her parents divorced when she was nine and she took some real blows to her self-esteem. She distrusted most men, gave up her dreams of going to college, had two divorces of her own, and struggled with money most of her life.

Her overprotectiveness of me was her desire that I avoid the hard knocks and land in a life of luxury. That's why getting my own college degree and marrying well were so important to her. Playing it safe with these moves would hedge my bets for getting the good life she felt she never had. As a young woman, I couldn't hear these motivations in her criticism—I just felt that she was too tough on me. Ironically, it took facing a few hard knocks of my own for me to understand my mother's need to protect me in this way.

My friend Nancy was raised very differently but experienced a similar sense of overprotectiveness. Her parents were older, quite wealthy, with the time to devote to raising their children abroad. She had a great childhood, with lots of travel, but spent so much time with her mother that she felt "squashed, overprotected, put under the microscope." "We became our mother's projects," she confided.

Because she was raised in Europe, her parents were more old-world in their thinking and treated her very differently from her brothers. "It was like I had a collar on me and was fetched like a dog because I was female, and my brothers were allowed to do anything they liked because they were boys. I always felt that if I had a penis, my mother would accept me."

Her brothers were given authority over her by her parents and were asked to drive her places and chaperone her on outings. Her brothers made matters worse by criticizing her to her parents and controlling her in their absence. "My brothers controlled my father, my father controlled my mother, and my mother controlled me. I was at the bottom of the feeding chain," she complained.

Because she had devoted so much time to shaping Nancy's life, her mother became overly critical of Nancy's life choices. She didn't approve of Nancy's being a model, but wanted her to come home and go to college instead. And when Nancy married a young man who was building his fortune, instead of one who already had a fortune, her mother was disappointed and put pressure on the couple to maintain the same privileged lifestyle Nancy had enjoyed as a child.

Nancy used to try convincing her mother that she and her husband were indeed building the life she wanted for them, but her mother wouldn't accept this, and it only made the relationship worse. So Nancy has chosen instead to go about the business of living her life as she sees fit, knowing that for the time being there is no pleasing her mother. She hopes that someday her mother will back off and get it.

If you have an overprotective mother, your challenge is to cut your mother's apron strings and still stay connected to her in the relationship. You must learn how to be more self-reliant, even if the messages you get from your mother are telling you that you can't make it on your own. It's a tricky dance, and can feel a bit like walking a tightrope: too much this way and you are under her control, too much that way and you have broken the connection with her.

There are some things you can do to make this dance easier for yourself:

- Break the habit of bringing all your problems to your mother. This only feeds her desire to protect you.
- Be more selective when you ask for your mother's advice.
- Act more and talk less. When your mother sees the results of your actions, she'll have evidence that you are getting the good life she wants for you.
- Put your mother's overprotective nature to better use by giving her a new job description in your life. Let her house-sit, watch your kids, keep your pets for the week, or do some other project where she can put her caretaker skills to use. Busy with these tasks, she may not have time to hover over your every move.

In an interview in US magazine, Jodie Foster explained how she likes to take her mother to expensive restaurants where her mother can order fancy hors d'oeuvres and then complain about how the restaurant prepares them. "This is the perfect position for her. She doesn't actually have to do anything, but she gets to be critical and judgmental about it while she's eating her smoked salmon."

Giving your mother a new job description is a powerful way to redirect

*her critic. Let her criticize the smoked salmon instead of you—now that's
peace!*

EMOTIONAL NEEDINESS

If your mother's motivation for criticizing you is emotional neediness, she is unhappy with her life and relationships and may be masking her insecurity in one
or more addictions. She is using criticism to stay connected to you and using
you to crutch her own life.

Linda says her mother, who was an alcoholic, was the master of verbal abuse. Her mother was a very accomplished career woman during
the day, but would lose it when she came home and started drinking.
Because she was emotionally unavailable to raise her own family, she
became very dependent on Linda to keep things together and was re-
lentless in criticizing her daughter. "No matter what I said or did, it was
never good enough," Linda shared.

Linda did what she could to distance herself from her mother and
the criticism. She adopted another family, spending as much time as
she could there, even staying overnight to be in a calmer environment.
In school she got top grades and was elected class president. But every
day when her mother drank, the cycle would start again. The criticism
was the only way her mother knew to stay connected to her daughter.

Years later, when Linda was an adult, she was in the Highlands Program, a values and skills-assessment course, and was asked to do a class
assignment of interviewing her parents. She was terrified to contact her
mother, because they hadn't spoken in years, but she finally found her
and interviewed her on the phone. The questions were designed to be
neutral and nonthreatening to her mother—she could not discuss her
own childhood or her mother's parenting as these subjects would be too
emotional.

The experience of interviewing her mother was so great that Linda
was able to heal much of her past pain. She said that in listening without judgment to her mother's lost dreams and life experiences, she was
able to feel compassion and love for her mother again.

Linda followed up that interview by visiting her mother in Costa Rica. It wasn't as if her mother was instantly emotionally available. "I saw my mother at her worst and best in a three-day period," she confessed. "One day, she thought I took her keys. She screamed and went out of control and was going to pull my hair, but she stopped. I immediately left and told her I wasn't coming back. She called me up and apologized, which she had never done before, and I realized she recognized what she had done. This was a major breakthrough in our relationship."

No longer the helpless child, Linda took care of herself when her mother lost emotional control and through healing this outburst and spending time together, both she and her mother became closer. Linda remains committed to staying in a relationship with her mother, but also maintaining her own emotional well-being.

If you were raised by an emotionally needy mother, you may feel like Linda that you missed much of your childhood and adolescence because your mother was always intruding in your life. That's why it's more important than ever for you to protect your own emotional well-being. You do not have to write your mother off, but you do need to tread more carefully in your interactions with her, because she simply isn't capable of doing things differently.

There are some things you can do to safeguard your own well-being:

- Adjust your expectations of your mother by understanding she cannot emotionally be there for you.
- Excuse yourself from the room or change the subject if the conversation becomes too emotionally draining.
- Say things like, "I'm sure you'll figure out what's best for you," encouraging your mother to solve her own problems.
- Refuse to take your mother's emotional bait when she says things like, "Don't let me upset you or ruin your day." Let her comment drop, or say, "You won't," and put your mother's funk back on her.

CONTROL

If your mother's unconscious motivation for criticizing you is control, it means she is out of control (overwhelmed, fearful, anxious) herself. Criticizing you is her way of trying to regain control over her own life.

Valerie calls her mother the ultimate control freak. She and her brothers and sisters weren't allowed to watch TV, listen to the radio, go to movies, have friends over. They had to leave their bedroom doors open and couldn't even find safe islands of privacy in their own home. Valerie even had to show her mother evidence of her menstrual periods and tell her when they started.

Her mother was a woman of extremes . . . a talented, free-spirited artist and a member of an ultraconservative religious group. She had always been a critical mother, a tough parent to live with, but after a serious car accident, she became even more impossible. Her mood swings were more extreme, and she was out of control with her own kids.

When Valerie was nineteen years old and still living at home, she wanted to interview for a job as a makeup artist at a prestigious health spa in Los Angeles. Her mother was so opposed to this life change that she told Valerie that if she insisted on interviewing for the job, she could no longer live at home. Valerie considered her options and decided to go ahead with the interview.

The night before she was supposed to leave, her mother, with her father's help, held her captive in the family's home. She cut the phone lines and proceeded to scream criticism at Valerie until two in the morning. It was as if the floodgates had opened, and her mother poured out a lifetime of criticism in one night.

Eventually, Valerie escaped and went to the interview. Her mother followed through on her threats. She changed the locks on the doors and forbade Valerie to come home. She never said she was sorry for what she had said or done.

Valerie still remembers that traumatic night as the event that broke her. Until that point, she had survived her mother's verbal tirades, but this was more than she could bear.

Finally away from her mother, Valerie went out of control herself and began to drink heavily. "I tried to look for love in the bottle, on the dance floor . . . but it wasn't there," she confided. Engaged several times, she never married. The thought of a safe intimate relationship was too scary for her.

How did Valerie find her way back to herself and her mother? It was her intense desire and commitment to end her mama drama. "There comes a point where you want to be done," she confessed. It took years of her own work, a twelve-step program for her alcoholism, a deep prayer life, and volunteer work with abused children to bring her own life back into control. By surrendering to God and serving others, she had found a new basis for rebuilding her relationship with her mother.

Today, she says she has truly forgiven her mother for the pain of the past and enjoys a more peaceful relationship with her. "If you can't make your way to peace with your mother, you won't have the peace yourself," she shares.

Valerie's story may seem more extreme than most, but the feelings are no less intense when you're being criticized by a controlling mother. It is as if you are being held hostage by her hurtful words and don't know how to escape.

If you feel your mother's motivation for criticizing you is control, you may want to try some of these alternative ways of relating to her:

- Recognize that your mother's control makes you feel out of control, and resist the urge to control back.
- Stop announcing and explaining your decisions, because this gives your mother something to try to control.
- Ignore your mother's unsolicited advice, or thank her for it, and still make the decision that's best for you.
- Decide to stay calm, no matter how out of control your mother gets, and not jump into the chaos with her.

Understanding the Nature of Attacks— Perceived vs. Real

With a new understanding of your mother's underlying motivations for criticism, your next challenge is to deal with the criticism itself, and to do this, you must understand something about the nature of attacks. When a perceived attack comes toward you, your first reaction is to defend yourself, yet it is your counterattack, not your mother's perceived attack, that is the more real of the two. By fighting back, you make your mother's attack real, when the attack is faulty to begin with.

PERCEIVED VS. REAL ATTACK

In aikido we learn not to move in anticipation of the attack but as soon as the real attack starts. The reason for this is quite simply that we might put ourselves in a more harmful position for the real attack. Since it isn't real yet, we can't know how to effectively move out of the way or neutralize our opponent. In fact, our moving first may cause our opponent to choose a different technique for which we are even less prepared.

When dealing with your mother, it is wasted effort and just plain foolish to try to defend yourself against a perceived attack, one that hasn't happened yet, or an attack based on a faulty assumption. It's much easier to hear the emotion behind the attack and redirect it or sidestep the conflict altogether. And you must remember that your choice of what you tell your mother to begin with will directly affect the kinds of comments you get back.

MAMA DRAMA MINUTE

I once dug myself in a hole when I defended myself against my mother's criticism that I was "too old" at age thirty-three to ride in a seventy-five-mile bike race. The perceived attack was faulty to begin with ... there were many riders much older than I who could easily ride the same course. I had trained with more experienced riders and knew my own strength and capabilities. I had set a realistic goal of finishing the course in eight hours or less, a good goal for a novice rider such as myself. I didn't need my mother's approval or permission to do this race.

But there I was vehemently defending my age, my right to do this, when my mother slam-dunked me with another attack that "I should stay home and have a baby." If I'd have listened to her "too old" comment and responded a different way, I could have saved us both some grief. By fighting back, I created more resistance, something for her to push against, and she blindsided me with another attack that I was even less prepared to defend.

In the bike race conflict, I had the following options, and probably more that I couldn't think of at the time:

- I could have blended with her "too old" comment and said something like, "You know about us old people, we're stubborn and set in our ways. No use trying to talk me out of doing this race." I actually think my mother would have gotten a good laugh out of this and let it go.
- I could have given the "no-response response" and just ignored her comment. Where could she go with that?
- I could have waited to tell her about the race until after I finished it and not given her the power to judge my doing it in the first place.
- I could have kept my accomplishment to myself and not told her about it at all.

These were all alternatives to digging in and fighting with her. The trick is dropping the emotion, seeing these options, and choosing one that empowers you *while you're in the conflict.*

Honoring Each Other's Vulnerabilities

On the mat, we learn to notice our partners' strengths and weaknesses and blend with both to create harmony. For example, a partner may have a more advanced rank than us or might be a beginner, and then we must adjust our techniques accordingly, based on our partners' ability to handle the falls associated with the techniques. Our partners may also have physical limitations we have to honor: lower-back problems, a sore shoulder, a weak knee, and we need to learn how to move with these limitations.

Because we are connected in our techniques, we develop an ability to sense openings with each other—where one of us wants to come into the other's space, where we feel the most vulnerable, where we are holding tension and need to let go. We know these things about each other yet must find ways to become one and move together in the technique. The best way to describe this mind-set is we are both simultaneously aware and honoring of each other's vulnerabilities.

As mothers and daughters we each come to the relationship with our own set of vulnerabilities. The question becomes, "Will we go for each other's jugular?" or "Will we adjust our techniques accordingly and learn to move with each other in ways that create more harmony instead of conflict?"

As daughters our weakness may be perceiving everything our mothers say and do as an attack and bracing ourselves accordingly. We become our own worst enemies, so rigid and entrenched in our positions that we stand in the way of the love we want. As mothers our weakness may be not seeing our daughters as grown-up women capable of making their own decisions and mistakes. We are tempted to criticize our daughters for their own good and lose the very love and respect we want from them. Coming from our weaknesses leaves us both feeling sad and unfulfilled, wondering where the love and honoring went.

Just because we know each other's vulnerabilities doesn't mean we have to take advantage of them. Instead, we can learn to move with each other's limitations and enjoy a more joyful relationship.

Sometimes, we sense an opening with each other, and we don't know how to move with it. We may feel so uncomfortable with the silence that we have a tendency to rush in and try to make something happen in our relationship. To avoid this trap, we must be able to stop and feel the silence without feeling the need to fill it. That's when it becomes important again to draw on our own quieting practice (prayer, meditation, walks) and our own power of intuition to reassure ourselves that it is indeed all right to be with the silence. Unless we stop and feel it and allow it into our lives, we may always find ourselves pushing it away, and it is this silence that mirrors the peace, the very feeling of harmony we are trying to create with our mothers.

Jane told me an interesting story about how she and her mother filled the silence. Her mother had loaned Jane some money, and when Jane didn't respond to her calls on her time schedule, she sent Jane a nasty card telling her she must not have appreciated the help. At the same time Jane had sent her mother a beautiful card thanking her for the loan. Their cards literally crossed in the mail. Jane hadn't called her mother back because there was a three-hour time difference and she had been extra busy with her business and family.

Talk about a misunderstanding! When Jane received the card from her mother, she was hurt and angry. Things had been going better in their relationship, and now her mother was criticizing her again. Jane called her mother and confronted her on her motivations for lending her the money, "Did you lend it to me because you wanted to help me or because you wanted something from me?" Her mother changed her tune and backed off.

Her mother had an opening (Jane wasn't calling and there was a space) and she filled it with criticism. Jane had an opening (she wasn't able to get back to her mother and there was a space) and she filled it with love and appreciation. We have the same choices, whether to fill the openings with more conflict or more love.

Notice that Jane didn't ruin her relationship over getting a hurtful card from her mother. It was appropriate for her to confront her mother on the issue of lending money with strings attached, but she still stayed in the relationship, a relationship that has deepened and evolved over the years.

Moving from a Culture of Criticism to a Culture of Respect

In the movie *Pretty Woman* Vivian tells Edward that her mother always called her a "bum magnet," because she had a talent for attracting losers. At that moment, he lovingly reassures her that she is indeed special, to which she replies, "But why is it always easier to believe the bad stuff?" Yes, why indeed?

In the shadow of our mothers' criticism, we may not be able to hear or receive the good stuff. We want to believe it, but we can't trust it because we have bought into all the negativity, and think we are somehow bad, unworthy. Our challenge is to get past the anger and criticism and to keep the hope that the good stuff can truly come from our mothers.

Critical mothers focus more on the result, what we did wrong, than our talents, strengths, or personal growth. Because this is their focus, it is difficult for them to give us that compliment or word of encouragement. Difficult, but not impossible—our mothers just may surprise us.

I have spoken with women from other cultures who wonder why I'm writing about mother-daughter conflict because it virtually doesn't exist in their countries. Lee, a woman from Vietnam, told me that children there are taught to respect their mothers as honored elders. They are simply not allowed by the family and society at large to stand face-to-face and criticize their mothers.

The mothers are very loving and nurturing and use discipline to teach this respect. If a child misbehaves, the mother spanks her on the bottom with a small stick, but first the mother must explain what the child has done wrong and why she is being punished. The mother does not hit with the hand . . . this is considered too personal and a form of abuse.

The culture makes a clear distinction between discipline and abuse. Sometimes the mothers ask their daughters to turn away and face the wall in silence. This punishment encourages the daughter to reflect on her actions and come back to her mother later. It is also a way for the daughter to maintain her dignity or "save face." She is not belittled or criticized in front of her peers and elders, but disciplined so that she may learn respect.

SAVING FACE

Saving face is an oriental concept that means tempering your words and actions so that you do not strip a person of her dignity or reputation in front of others. It is important that you don't become overly critical of yourself and others by allowing your mother's criticism of you to enrage your own critic. Practice saving face in all your relationships and you will experience more peace.

Lee explained that in America, mothers and daughters have "too much freedom," a freedom that is misused to criticize and hurt each other. She didn't experience problems with her mother, but said she felt caught between two cultures when she was raising her daughter here. Refusing to follow the old ways, her daughter became selfish and demanding and began criticizing Lee for not buying her enough expensive things like her American friends had. Lee feels our culture supports criticism and disrespect towards mothers.

Her point about too much freedom is well taken. Our culture seems to tolerate much more conflict and violence than some other cultures do. Maybe it never occurred to us that it could be any other way. Maybe we can learn something from this concept of "saving face."

Creating the relationship we want with our mothers, relationships built on mutual trust and honor, is an important step toward building a culture of respect in this country. We may think our relationships won't make a difference, but they will. They will serve as inspirational examples for relationships in the future and drop a different paradigm into the pipeline for the mothers and daughters who come after us.

Mother-Daughter Body Drama:

Rewriting Your Body Script

They say I'm built just like my mother. I think she planned

it that way, because now she can borrow all my clothes.

Martha's Story: Weighing In for Her Mother

"The summer I was nineteen, I went to a fat camp for Jewish girls," Martha said. "I called it Camp Lake of the Blintzes. They had locks on the refrigerators, and I don't mean the kind you put on bagels. They gave us such small amounts of food, we had to snack on ice.

"I was the oldest of five kids, the shortest and the fattest. No other brother or sister had a weight problem. I was taking singing lessons at the time, and my mother would shame me about my weight by saying, 'Sophie Tuckers are out' or 'You have such a pretty face—if only we could see your facial structure.' "

Martha's mother made her weigh in on a regular basis. "The scale was in my mother's bedroom, I used to lean against her dresser to make myself weigh less. When she found this out, she moved the scale to the middle of the room, and I had to weigh in there. She really didn't want a fat kid." To make matters worse, Martha's maiden name was Fink and the kids in school used to taunt her with comments like, "Rat Fink" and "Fat Fink."

By the time Martha was thirteen, she was put on diet pills and didn't stop taking them until she was in her twenties. Her fat-farm visit got her down to a size 8/9, but weight would continue to be a struggle for her most of her adult life.

At this point she internalized her mother's critic and began drinking. "When you were brought up with constant criticism about who you were and what you looked like, you'd do anything to make yourself feel better. Drinking made me feel prettier, sexier, smarter." Her drinking continued well into her thirties.

Martha decided to become sober when her daughter was five years old, because she saw herself, under the influence of alcohol, repeating the same negative patterns with her daughter that she had experienced with her mother. "When I stopped medicating myself with alcohol, I had to face my feelings. I looked at myself in the mirror and realized I had choices to make. I could continue to blame my mother, feel sorry for myself, and play the victim, or I could look at my participation in the dynamic between us."

With the help of a twelve-step recovery program and group therapy, Martha became painfully honest with herself and began to look at both core patterns with her mother and also some of her underlying core beliefs. She realized one of her patterns was to hurt her mother first before her mother hurt her, and she stopped doing this. Martha realized that deep inside she believed that she didn't really matter, and often treated her mother as if she didn't matter either. She understood that these patterns and beliefs were her way of protecting that fat little girl inside her that was so traumatized by weighing in, and she learned to forgive herself and her mother for the past. She found that when she changed, her relationship with her mother began to change.

Martha's mother battled various cancers over a twenty-three-year period. Once Martha became sober and more honest with herself, she was able to deal with her mother more directly, to see the goodness in their relationship, and tell her, "I want you to know you've been a good mother," before she died. To her surprise, her mother came clean, too, and apologized for some of the things she had done to Martha.

When her mother died, Martha sang a perfect rendition of "That's What Friends Are For" at her funeral, a cappella in front of two hundred people, and realized how much she loved singing. That performance was the inspiration for developing her one-woman comedy show, "Yes I Kahn." "When I was young, I was performing for my mother's approval and love, and now I do it for God, for Spirit, for myself," she explained. "You can only do that when you get to the point of forgiveness."

Forgiving her mother has allowed Martha to be kinder to herself and her body and to change her relationship with her daughter. She has been sober for years and continues to take steps to improve her health and well-being, like practicing tai chi. She admits she is still twenty pounds overweight and doesn't feel as good about her body as she would like, but at least now she can pass a store window or mirror, see her reflection, and think, "That woman looks pretty," and that woman is her. To this day, she doesn't have a scale in her house—it's just too painful of a reminder of those weigh-ins with her mother.

Inheriting a Negative Body Script from Our Mothers

Like Martha, we may have inherited negative body messages from our mothers that are affecting the choices we make with our bodies. These messages, and the way our mothers treated their own bodies, have made up *underlying body scripts* that we carry with us. Our mothers influence this body script in a number of ways:

- Our taste in food
- Our use/restriction of drugs
- Our weight
- Our acceptance of our bodies
- Our grooming
- Our choice of clothing
- Our beliefs about our sexuality
- Our ability to nurture ourselves
- Our relationships with men

A CRAVING FOR FATTY FOODS

My mother was a former beauty queen, very beautiful, and now she weighs over three hundred pounds. I have always struggled with weight loss and am very hard on myself about my body. I remember my mother eating fatty foods like chips in the middle of the night, and I have the same craving for fatty foods. I have binged on these foods, especially through life changes, and hated myself afterward. —Linda

---

DRAMA TRAP: ACTING OUT THE NEGATIVE MESSAGES

You may find yourself acting out the negative body messages: hating certain body parts, struggling with weight loss, fighting addictions, or being more sexually promiscuous because of the body drama you experienced with your mother.

This body script is also made up of the unconscious messages and/or vows we've made about our mothers and our bodies: "My mother is fat and I'm never going to look like her," or "My mother looks hot—I hope I can be as beautiful and sexy as she is," or "I'm so mad at my mother, I just want to eat." These are the true demons that get us to stuff our faces in anger or kill ourselves in workouts at the gym.

It's important to remember here that our mothers are not consciously trying to hurt us. They are simply sharing their body scripts, which may or may not have worked for them, scripts they may have inherited from their own mothers. Indeed there may be many valuable

influences we wish to incorporate into our lives. But unless we understand and change our mothers' negative influences on our body scripts,
we are doomed to repeat our body drama until we complete it.

*I remember a pivotal time in my relationship with mother when I was
twelve years old that changed my attitude toward food and my body. At the
time, I competed with my brothers by eating as much as they did, and I was
physically active enough that this didn't hurt my body. Then my mother
said, "If you keep eating like that, you'll end up being just as fat and ugly
as I was." I was so upset by her comment, I thought, "Screw you! I'm going
to do what I want." Food had never been an emotional issue, but after this
comment, I continued to overeat just to get back at my mother. By the time
I was fourteen years old and puberty had set in, I was just as fat as she
had been at that age, and not feeling good about myself. My rebellion, my
reverse psychology, had backfired on me, and I still struggle with my
weight.*   —Erin

Modeling (or imitating) our mothers' behavior with their bodies is
the most powerful influence on the way we treat our bodies. When we
were babies, the first action we took after our first breath involved eating, rooting for our mothers' breasts. By the time we were two years
old, most of our eating behaviors had already been modeled by our
mothers long before we even had the language to discuss them. Over
the years we continued to base our relationships with food, sex, and our
own bodies on the relationships we saw modeled by our mothers.

If our mothers referred to our first menstrual periods as "the curse,"
we may have found ourselves suffering from more cramps and complications with our periods. If our mothers were hounding us about
having babies and we were still feeling traumatized by our own childhoods, we may have experienced problems with infertility. If our mothers were starving themselves or bingeing or flaunting their sexuality, we
picked up on those patterns. All those messages were very powerful.

I remember some childhood friends of mine whose mother was
upset about getting older. The mother would wear tight, sexy clothes
and lots of makeup to look as young as possible. This set the stage for

some unconscious competition between the mother and her daughters, who were beautiful in their own right. Instead of enjoying their fresh, natural good looks, these daughters went for the same heavy made-up look their mother had modeled for them. And to keep up with her mother, one daughter became sexually active and pregnant in her teens.

Why We Self-Medicate with Food and Alcohol Around Our Mothers

When we were babies, we'd react to a stimulus (a noise, light, messy diaper, thirst, or hunger) by crying to our mothers for immediate comfort. A light would come on, and our mothers would give us a warm bottle or breast and a change, and all was well. We had that warm fuzzy feeling and knew we would survive for a few more hours.

Thirty years later we're sitting alone in the darkness watching the Late Show, stuffing our faces with food, and we're still looking for that same warm, fuzzy feeling. From infancy on, we have learned to use food (and beverages) to medicate ourselves to relieve our anxiety.

During the initial stages of acute anxiety, we are so stressed out, our bodies go into fight-or-flight mode, locking up our digestion. Our mouths become dry, and we can't produce enough gastric juices to digest our food. We subconsciously learn that when we eat or drink something, we force our digestion to start up again, and therefore eating becomes soothing to our bodies (and emotions).

What feels the most satisfying to us in these moments of high anxiety is eating carbohydrates, simple sugars which give us an immediate buzz (a rise in our blood sugar) and a plateau period, which tranquilizes us from the anxiety—but this is short-lived, because our moods soon come crashing down again and we have to keep medicating ourselves with food to feel buffered from our mothers.

Add to this the dynamic that we daughters have spent much of our

initial bonding with our mothers around food, and we begin to understand why food has such power over our relationships with our mothers. We all spent countless hours with our mothers in the kitchen
helping them prepare everyday and holiday meals. Whenever we had
a problem, it was probably discussed with with our mothers at the
kitchen table over a glass of milk and a plate of cookies or some other
favorite snack. If we watched a movie with our mothers, they probably
made us their special buttered popcorn. If we were upset over a
boyfriend, our mothers probably fed us a piece of chocolate cake to
make us feel better.

Over the years we may have done this so much that we developed an
obsessive-compulsive pattern with food and our mothers. Whenever
our mothers upset us, we began to obsess over the problem so much
that we couldn't shake our thoughts. Our anxiety grew to such a point
that we felt trapped in the problem. Our compulsive (impulsive) act
then became eating as a way to escape our discomfort and soothe our
bodies and emotions.

MAMA DRAMA MINUTE

I remember going home to see my mother, who was quite overweight, and
having her tell me that I was too thin, that it was her job to fatten me up.
And being the dutiful daughter, I binged on her M&M jar, and the cookies and
cakes she baked, and I gained five pounds or more each visit. Here I was a
grown woman, still trying to please my mother by overeating, instead of confronting her with my thinness.

Because going home meant conflict with my mother, I began medicating myself with food as soon as I stepped into her house. I was feeding my feelings,
instead of feeding my hunger, and hurting my body in the process.

When we self-medicate with food and alcohol, we are numbing ourselves to our true feelings about our mothers and using it as a means of
avoiding conflict. Carried to an extreme, this overeating can cause us
to become just as fat as our mothers so we can gain their love and approval again.

If our mothers are overweight themselves, they may have a secret desire to see us fail in rewriting our body scripts, because our failure somehow justifies their failure or excuses, and they don't have to face their own body issues. All I had to do was walk through the door, and my thinness would confront my mother. It took away all her excuses that "the women in our family are heavy," especially when I got to be older and was still thin.

Gaining weight to be like our mothers can be a trap, a mixed message. On the one hand, we may feel we have their love and approval, but on the other hand, the weight may make us feel more mature and sexually developed for our age, and we don't want to get our mothers mad at us for attracting our fathers' sexual attention. We feel conflicted at best.

How Cultural Standards Affect
Mother-Daughter Body Drama

We can't intelligently discuss rewriting our own body scripts until we address this impossible cultural standard of ours that keeps us chasing the ideal of anorexic beauty. Nowhere is this more apparent than with the changing statistics of our centerfolds and beauty queens. Dr. William H. Polonsky, Assistant Professor of Psychiatry at the University of California–San Diego, stated in his seminar, "Personality, Motivation, and Health," that "the average height and body weight of *Playboy* centerfolds and winners of the Miss America pageant went from approximately 5´2˝ and 140 pounds in 1964 to 5´9˝ and 109 pounds in 1995."

The message to us is "Be tall, maybe even taller than your genetic blueprint calls for, and thin, thirty pounds thinner to be exact—or we won't find you attractive." So we go out and buy the platform shoes, get the body wraps to lose inches, and pour ourselves into tight, uncomfortable dresses, trying to live up to this ideal. No wonder my Israeli girlfriend joked, "American women suffer for beauty."

Our teenage daughters especially suffer. They have a fantasy image of what their bodies should look like, and if their hips are too big or their breasts are too small, they feel bad about themselves. And this body imaging gets worse and more self-abusive the older they get.

Lynne Nieto, RN, MSN, Certified Eating Disorders Specialist, and Psychiatric Nurse Practitioner with Lindora Medical Clinics in California (see Resources Sections) sees twenty to thirty clients a day who want to lose weight, many of them teenagers or young women who only want to lose the five to ten pounds to get to their ideal weight. These women often go to doctors who tell them, "Just push yourself away from the table," as if it were no big deal. This concerns Lynne because she knows from her own experience that these young women will find other ways to lose the weight, things like fen-fen and liquid-protein diets that could put their very lives at risk. She would rather have them in her program where they can be medically and psychologically evaluated for safe weight loss.

Because this quest for the perfect body doesn't go away, mothers must be aware of the mixed messages they are giving their daughters and pay attention to the way their daughters are treating their bodies. Yet, according to Lynne, mothers often take one of two approaches. Either they ignore their daughters' pleas, behaviors, and concerns to shape their bodies to an ideal, or they compete with their daughters in a two-way drama with their own preoccupation over weight, size, and sexiness. Neither of these responses will help their daughters, because the mothers either deny there's a problem or become a part of the same anorexic standard their daughters are chasing.

Why is it important for us to understand this? Because we have to hear whatever our mothers tell us about losing weight in the context of this centerfold mentality, and forgive her and ourselves for buying into it. The weight prejudice is simply greater than both of us.

What can we do? We can understand this prejudice and help ourselves and our daughters set more realistic goals for lasting change.

We can be kinder to ourselves, spend less time on reckless diets and more time accepting our bodies the way they are.

Avoiding Extremes: Starving Ourselves Or Staying Our Mothers' Fat Little Girls

Just as we tend to swing to extremes with our mothers' criticism, we tend to live extremes with our bodies, either starving ourselves to get their attention or staying their fat little girls to get their approval. When this happens, even losing five pounds is serious business, because we must face what's really going on with our mothers, our fears of being consumed or abandoned by them, and these fears can feel like life or death to us, especially when we feel incapable of expressing ourselves around our mothers to begin with. So instead of telling her our pain, we mistreat our bodies to get her attention.

A DAUGHTER'S CRY FOR HELP

An eating disorder such as bulimia can be the daughter's cry for help, her way of expressing rage at her mother that she feels she can't express in the relationship. In this way bulimia becomes her language, her method of getting her mother's attention and communicating to the outside world.

Julie was at one extreme, using her bulimia to get her mother's attention. "I just wish my mother would notice me," she confided to Lynne. She came to Lindora ten pounds overweight, but wanting to lose twenty-five pounds to get to her ideal fantasy weight.

Because her father left when she was two years old, her relationship with her mother was even more intense, and her mother was so emotionally needy that Julie felt she was becoming the parent. She wanted to separate from the demands her mother put on her, but at the same time she didn't want to abandon her. So instead of being able to express this to her mother, she started expressing it through her body.

Julie wouldn't let Lindora control her weight loss, but started bingeing and vomiting in an effort to regain control over her own life. She refused to follow the treatment team's recommendations, including therapy, and was eventually referred out to other doctors specializing in bulimia, at which time she left Lindora.

She returned to Lindora three years later, to lose the same ten pounds she had started to lose before, but this time she had stopped the bulimia and was finally dealing with the underlying mother issues of her body drama. Through studying psychology in college and going to her own counselor, she learned to detach from her mother's emotional neediness and take care of herself. She was finally ready to rewrite her body script and set more realistic goals of weight loss without all the emotional baggage.

Teresa was on the opposite extreme of body drama with her mother. Instead of losing weight, as her mother wanted her to do, she embraced her fat because it made her feel like more of a woman.

Teresa's father brought Teresa, her mother, and her sister to Lindora to lose weight. At the time, Teresa was twelve years old and weighed at 160 pounds, twice the weight of her twin sister, who was the only thin female in the family.

The fact that Teresa's mother was overweight herself played greatly into the dynamics of their relationship. Her mother would take Teresa shopping with her twin, and Teresa would be upset because she had to buy clothes that were so much bigger than her sister's. This was her way of pressuring Teresa to be thin, something she also wanted for herself, but this only made Teresa more competitive, more determined to cling to her fat because she was more sexually developed than her sister. Teresa's mother was unable to lose weight herself, so she sent mixed messages to Teresa: be thin like your sister—be fat, be a woman, like me.

By clinging to her fat, Teresa was able to get her mother's and father's attention and express the power she felt helpless to express in other ways. Her determination not to lose weight was her way of getting back at her parents. Her mother and sisters became her allies in this power play, as they refused to lose weight as well.

The health professionals at Lindora realized that until the family dynamics were addressed, nothing was going to change for these women, so they offered the family a full refund, gave them a counseling referral, and suggested they come back at a later time.

For things to change, Teresa would have to find other ways than her fat to express herself with her parents. Her overweight mother and sister would have to face their own weight problems and stop focusing on Teresa. Her mother would have to surrender the illusion that her twins are the same and accept that they truly are different. The thin sister would have to risk her princess position in the family and realize that she is part of the problem. And the father would have to deal with his own power issues, with the fact that he really doesn't have the control over his family he thinks he does.

In Julie's case her fear of abandoning her mother was the main motivator in starving her body, and in Teresa's case, her fear of being consumed by her mother's (and father's) power was the motivator for clinging to her fat. Both young women chose extreme measures with their bodies in lieu of confronting their mothers.

When we look at these stories, we cannot help but see that choosing the path of least resistance can be damaging to our own health and well-being. If we've inherited body scripts that create that much pain in our lives, we must be willing to change them before they kill us.

Breaking with Mother's Sex Script

When Nancy was a little girl, she asked her mother, "Where do babies come from?" Her mother explained sex in a very clinical way, and added, "Sex is for the man, not the woman. Only the man gets pleasure."

At the time, Nancy was already masturbating on a daily basis, enjoying her body and wondering if something was wrong with her or if
she was going to hurt herself. "I wondered if my mother and father had
tried what I was doing, and I decided I wasn't going to stop having sex
with myself because it felt so good."

As Nancy grew up, she didn't feel the need to be promiscuous, but
did choose a man with whom she could fully express herself sexually
and married him in her early twenties. She loves holding hands with
him, rubbing his leg, kissing him, and isn't afraid to express her affection openly in front of others. Nancy's mother is disgusted with these
displays of affection and wonders what happened to her daughter to
make her like sex.

Even as a young child Nancy knew that her mother's messages about
sex were off base, and she boldly allowed herself to believe and try
something different. If she had grown up believing that sex was only for
the man's pleasure, she would have never discovered the beautiful and
sensuous woman inside her. Changing the sex script she inherited from
her mother became essential to her own growth and development as a
woman.

How did Nancy break from her mother's sex script? She compared
her mother's negative message with her own experience of sex and decided that her mother's message was untrue. She continued with her
practice of having sex with herself because this made her feel good
and put her in touch with her own sexuality. She made other life
choices, such as choosing a husband with whom she could fully express
herself sexually, which further reinforced her new beliefs about her
body. The result is she is happily married with a healthy sex life and a
much better outlook on sex than anyone else in her family.

We may have been raised with similar taboos on sex and have to ask
ourselves if those taboos are serving us now. There are good reasons
for mothers to talk to their daughters about abstinence and safe sex,
but too often they do so with a lot of misinformation or negative messages that can leave daughters ignorant or questioning their own sexuality.

Rewriting Your Body Script

Mother: "Clean your plate. There are starving children in Africa."
Daughter: "If I leave this much, how many kids will die?"

To rewrite our body scripts effectively, we must understand something about pain and pleasure, both powerful motivators for change. Too many times we are motivated by pain (what we don't want, what we want to avoid), and yet this motivator can set up a dynamic in which we rebel against the very things that are trying to help us and go back to our old patterns which may be more destructive, but are also more comfortable (pleasurable) to us.

This dynamic is precisely why most diets don't work, because they motivate us from restriction (pain) and reinforce what we can't have. One woman I interviewed described her diet as a "punitive exercise," "a recipe for a binge." We can only tolerate the pain so long before we start craving certain foods and snap back to eating what we used to eat because it makes us feel better.

This pain dynamic is equally ineffective in reframing our body messages from our mothers. If we are motivated to change by proving them wrong, by going against them, we may be doomed to snapping back to our old patterns, not because they are good for us, but because they feel more familiar to us, less painful than taking responsibility for our own bodies.

Once we understand these dynamics, we can see how rewriting our body scripts becomes more a matter of going towards pleasure with our bodies (what we want, what feels good, what serves our health and well-being) than going against the negative messages we may have inherited from our mothers. This is aikido in its purest form, going with what is, rather than fighting against it. It involves unscrambling the negative messages and vows and replacing them with new beliefs and practices that support us in getting the bodies and minds we want.

Much of our discussion to this point has been about unscrambling those messages:

- We know that our mothers may have had several negative influences on our body scripts or that we may have made vows around our mothers' comments and actions which created our own negative messages.
- We understand that we live in a culture that epitomizes anorexic beauty and we know how that plays into the equation.
- We remember that our mothers' criticism is more about them than us, that what they told us about our bodies was really the way they felt about their own bodies.
- We know from Julie's and Teresa's stories how important it is to handle the underlying emotional issues or we will sabotage our efforts for lasting change.

So how do you rewrite your body script? Desire. You have to want to do it because it's something that makes you feel good, not something that pleases your mother. If you try to do it for your mother or someone else, you will surely fail. To help you create that lasting change I'll be examining four areas:

- Developing Self-Knowledge About Your Body and Emotions
- Changing Your Relationship with Food
- Appreciating Your Body
- Uncovering the Total Woman Inside You

Developing Self-Knowledge About Your Body and Emotions

MAMA DRAMA MINUTE

Nowhere did my mother's and my beliefs on our bodies conflict more than during my struggle with infertility. When surgery and fertility drugs failed me, I turned to alternative medicine for some options. A chiropractor who specialized in nutrition suggested that I might have food allergies which were affecting my fertility and suggested a radical change in my diet—no dairy products, red meat, chicken, caffeine, chocolate, or alcohol.

Shortly after this consultation, I went home to visit my mother and wouldn't you know it, she took me to a smoky cocktail lounge for lunch. I was frantically looking for something I could eat and opted for a salad, but not before my mother had noticed everything on the menu I didn't order.

She wasted no time getting to the point. "So why aren't you eating steak, Denise?" she asked. I should have given her the short answer like, "I'm trying a change of diet," but as soon as I mentioned "chiropractor" and "no red meat" we were off and running. She reminded me that one of my cousins had a stroke on a chiropractor's table, that I should stay away from those quacks. She told me that I always had rich blood because of my solid beef diet, and she added that she herself had eaten red meat and became pregnant, so I should just drop this foolishness.

If I'd been smart, I would have stopped there and let "Dr. Mom" give her prognosis in peace. But when I told her I was getting weekly massages and could feel energy blockages release during these treatments and that I was taking yoga and knew when my body was in harmony and when it was not, this was more than she could stand.

She took a long drag on her cigarette and a sip of her Southern Comfort, and said, "So what do you mean you 'know' your body?" By now I was in a no-win situation and nothing I could say or do would convince her that I hadn't fallen off the deep end and "gone Californian" on her as she told one of her friends. Needless to say, I never mentioned "knowing my body" again.

When Martha stopped drinking, she was forced to pay attention to her body. When I went through my infertility, I had to do the same. Sometimes it takes a radical change in our bodies or health for us to wake up and pay attention to what's really happening to us, and this includes our thoughts and emotions as well.

One of the biggest deterrents to changing our body scripts is expecting that these changes will happen overnight. Change is a journey, not an event. It happens gradually, by noticing what feels good and what doesn't feel good with our bodies. It comes from maturity, from introspection, from asking ourselves some honest questions and giving ourselves some honest answers. It also comes from experiencing such practices as yoga and the martial arts, where we are asked to move more consciously within our bodies.

Jeannie had such resistance to exercising that she would think of every excuse to miss her workouts. She tried scheduling them in the morning, then didn't want to get out of bed to do them. She tried to schedule them at night, then was too tired to do them after work. Finally, her therapist told her that it was nonnegotiable, that she couldn't give herself those options. She decided to approach it in a way that made her feel in control. She told herself that she would try exercising consistently for a month, and if after that she didn't feel better, look better, and have more energy, she would give herself permission to stop.

It's important to note here that changing her body script was so anxiety-producing that every time she approached it, she felt trapped by her own decision, so she had to create a scenario where her decision seemed more open-ended (that she could quit after a month) for her to relax enough to start exercising. Once she did this, she felt safe enough to try her exercise program, and at the end of the thirty days, she felt and looked so much better she decided to continue it. It had already become habit, part of her new script, and she was able to continue it with less anxiety.

For you to make lasting changes in your body script, you must first pay attention to what you're doing with your body, what feels good and what hurts it, to what you're telling yourself about such things as food, exercise, alcohol, and sex. Once you understand your own personal dynamics, you must decide to take some actions outside of your normal routine and repeat those actions consistently enough until they become habit, part of your new script.

TRY THIS

Try keeping a body journal where you can write any thoughts and emotions about food, exercise, alcohol, and sex. I am not suggesting a food journal where you record all your meals and calories, because that will put you back into the high-anxiety mode of dieting. Just journal your body behaviors and messages (any insights or emotions that come to you while you're eating or drinking).

Say that you notice you drink too much wine every time you go out on a date. You've written in your journal that you seem nervous around your dates, that the only way you can seem to relax is by drinking lots of wine. You realize that this is a form of self-medicating, and you don't want to continue to do this, so you try some new moves:

- You decide to have one glass of wine, followed by a glass of iced tea to counteract the effects of the wine.
- You choose a new drink for your dates—mineral water with bitters and a twist of lime. This drink is light and chic and gives the appearance that you are having a cocktail when you really aren't. The amount of alcohol in the bitters is quite insignificant, but enough to make you feel like you're having a real drink.
- You decide to shorten your dates and plan a late-night rendevous with a girlfriend for coffee. That way you won't be tempted to overdrink.

- You decide to read a book or take a seminar on relationships so you can better understand dating dynamics.

The more you practice this focused introspection, followed by consistent action, the more successful you'll be in creating lasting change in your body script. Remember that it takes thirty days to change a habit and thirty days to reinforce it, so give yourself a trial period and then renew it for yourself to reinforce your changes.

Changing Your Relationship with Food—How to Stop Feeding Your Feelings

When you go home to visit your mother, you have to accept the fact that she and her food will be there waiting for you. You must be aware of your tendency to self-medicate and make a plan for a visit that's kinder to your body.

TRY THIS

- As much as possible, try to resolve your personal problems before you visit your mother. If you go home in crisis, you may have a tendency to overeat.
- Eat before you visit your mother, if it's just a short day visit.
- Know that you may overeat and compensate for this by taking walks or going to the local gym.
- Take your mother out to dinner at a restaurant you both like where you can order healthier food.
- Offer to shop and cook for your mother a few nights during your visit.

Hypnotherapist Fred Stemen sees many women who have failed miserably at diets and rather than take them back into diet thinking, which causes them more anxiety, he teaches them to change their relationship with food. *First he takes away the restrictions:* he tells them they can eat whatever they want in whatever amounts they want. His purpose here is not to have them gorge themselves to death, but to have them relax about food, so they can eventually select healthier food automatically for themselves. *Next, he isolates the relationship issues that are serving as the stimulus to eat.* He works on these relationships one by one, relieving the person's anxiety (and desire to self-medicate with food and alcohol) further. *Next, he works on improving the person's self-image.* Until these women can believe they can be thin, they will keep gaining the weight back because their beliefs have locked them into maintaining their weight at a certain level.

But most importantly, he teaches them to become *gourmet eaters,* to savor food, to eat to satisfy themselves, not to stuff emotions. He tells them if they really want a few ounces of a fattening sharp cheddar cheese, that they will not feel satisfied until they eat some, that they're better off eating a small quantity of this than a large quantity of another cheese that is less satisfying, but more fattening, to them.

When you take the time to slow down and savor your food, you will find yourself eating less and enjoying it more.

TRY THIS

To break the habit of eating unconsciously with emotion or other distractions, become a gourmet eater, determined to savor every bite:

- Sit down to eat (don't eat while standing or driving).
- Drop the distractions (TV, book).
- Buy and cook fresh foods that have more aroma and taste.
- Smell the food before eating it (take in the aromas).
- Avoid mixing foods on your fork (if something doesn't taste good by itself, don't eat it).
- Slowly chew each bite until the flavor is gone and then swallow.
- Create gourmet ambience in your kitchen or dining room with candles, flowers, music.

You may have to practice savoring your food, because you may be accustomed to using food to pacify yourself while you're doing something else (like paying your bills). But once you do practice it on a regular basis, you will find yourself snacking less because you have designated times to eat, and are naturally selecting healthier foods that taste better, and feel more satisfying.

How do you get to this natural selection of lighter and healthier foods? By noticing which foods make you feel good and which foods make you feel heavy or bloated. For example, if you were going out on a date, you would not choose to eat something like pork and beans or chicken-fried steak and mashed potatoes. These are not sexy date foods. Why? Because these foods are heavier and gaseous and would make you feel heavy. You would probably choose instead to eat something like a light salad, fish, or chicken. When you know your body and pay attention to how it feels after certain meals, you will eventually start to choose lighter foods that have more taste and make you feel better.

Jay Robb, author of *The Fat Burning Diet,* (see Resources Section) does something similar by giving his readers a variety of satisfying, fat-burning foods to choose from. He does suggest restricting certain fats and carbohydrates that inhibit your body's ability to burn fat, but there is still so much to choose from, you can easily feel satisfied on his diet. What is the payoff for you? You can burn fat anywhere—in your sleep, while you're shopping, while you're talking—as long as you're eating the right fat-burning foods.

Jay reminds his audiences that diet, not exercise, is the best fat-burner. Exercise is more for toning the muscles and conditioning the body and should be included in your routine (fifteen to thirty minutes of aerobics and fifteen to thirty minutes of weight training, three times a week), but it is not to be overdone, as too much exercise puts undue stress on your body. What you eat and how you eat make the most difference in getting the body you want.

Appreciating Your Body—Using the Mirror Fest Exercise
Most of us look in the mirror and immediately focus on what we don't like about our bodies, because we don't live up to the ideal centerfold.

We cover our bodies with bulky clothes or ask to make love in the dark because we just can't find the beauty in ourselves, let alone drink in every feature.

I remember reading Louise Hay's book, *Love Your Body*, and thinking how strange it seemed to have an affirmation for every part of the body. My brother even joked, "I just can't love my anus, Denise." It seemed totally ridiculous. But now that I realize the ways we violate ourselves in front of the mirror, I don't think it's strange at all.

Because this doesn't come naturally, you must have a mirror fest with yourself to break the old negative messages. You've learned to savor your food. Now it's time to savor your body.

TRY THIS: "MIRROR FEST EXERCISE"

The next time you get out of the shower, stand naked in front of your mirror and take a good look at yourself. Notice which of your features you immediately want to criticize. Notice which ones you immediately love. Don't just focus on the breasts and buttocks. Notice all the other subtle nuances that make you a woman: the shape of your ear lobes, the curve of your neck, the contours of your body. Buy a Kama Sutra box (see Resources Section) and play with the feather brush, the honey dust, the oils, the ointments. Repeat this process often until you can fully savor your body, drinking in every feature.

It is important to notice what kind of messages come up when you are doing this exercise. You may be surprised at how critical or how affirming you are of certain body parts. If you can't find anything you like, that's a big wake-up call that your body scripting is not supporting you and needs a radical overhaul.

There is a time to take an honest assessment of your body and make plans to tone and condition yourself, but this isn't one of those times. This is the time you take to celebrate who you are right now. The more you can be gentle with yourself and do this exercise, the more you'll be able to make other lasting changes in your body script, because you are sending yourself the subliminal message that you love your body and want to take care of it.

When you do come across a negative message, don't fight it, because what you resist persists. Instead let it go and keep focusing on what you like about your body. Soon you will begin to see yourself as a beautiful woman rather than a composite of body parts that are less than perfect.

TRY THIS

Now that you appreciate your body, take it on a shopping spree to Victoria's Secret. Go ahead, buy those thong bikinis you've always wanted. Try on the lace bustier, garter belt, and stockings. Throw out those flannel pajamas and buy yourself a sexy nightie.

A man once confided in me that he loves women who wear sexy lingerie for themselves, because it shows they have confidence in their sensuality and a sense of playfulness.

So go ahead, indulge yourself—I won't tell!

As the mirror fest exercise implies, we often get stuck focusing on the breasts and buttocks because these are the points that make us desirable or not desirable in men's eyes. The trap is we tend to think of ourselves as one-dimensional women, a composite of our body parts, instead of multifaceted women with a variety of needs and expressions. Is it little wonder then that we often settle for men who treat us like nothing more than sex objects?

W. Charisse Goodman writes about this preoccupation with our anatomy in her book, *The Invisible Woman: Confronting Weight Prejudice in America* (Gurze Books) (see Resources Section):

> . . . breasts are the only female body parts which are popularly considered more attractive with increasing size. It's also hard to escape that the physical feature most consistently celebrated in woman is that which feeds others. This attitude, combined with the more recent emphasis on a female physique that's tiny except in the chest, illuminates the cultural expectations that women provide others with boundless physical and psychological nur-

turing and pleasure while keeping their own needs and desires on a short, tight leash.

So in addition to the impossible standard of anorexic beauty, we've added big breasts to the equation, telling us once again, that if they don't literally measure up, we aren't as attractive. This message is sending thousands of women to their local plastic surgeons for liposuction, tummy tucks, butt lifts, and breast jobs, and some of them never make it back. A forty-something woman in Orange County, California, recently died from health complications while receiving liposuction. She was willing to risk her life to look good.

The danger with this plastic surgery craze is it keeps us focused on changing our body scripts externally, when it doesn't address the emptiness and unworthiness we may be feeling on the inside. If we started with our mothers' messages that our bodies didn't measure up, we will still carry those messages with us no matter what our cup size is, until we're willing to recognize the true message for what it is and let it go.

One woman I interviewed confided in me that her mother used to call herself "Tits," and her "Titty Baby" because her mother's breasts were larger than hers and because her mother said she needed to come home and get some tit (motherly advice) every once in a while. Talk about a negative body message! This woman's father and brother played along, teasing her with a makeshift bra of two Band-Aids and a string. As a teenager, she laughed, but inside she was hurt. She never felt good about her breasts and would stiffen up if a boy even brushed up against them. She attracted a boyfriend who called them "big blossoms" and married a husband who was obsessed with women with "big ones." She always wondered why her husband married her if he really wanted a woman with big breasts, until one of her friends very candidly asked her why she'd chosen a man who didn't think her body was beautiful the way it was.

The mother-daughter body drama around her breasts had influenced the way she saw herself, the worthiness she felt in choosing a husband. At one point, she purchased a set of subliminal tapes that were supposed to regress her to her adolescence, so her breasts could grow one cup size larger, but she didn't use them. She also considered going to a plastic surgeon for a new procedure to naturally enhance her breasts with her own body cells, but she decided against it. Instead, she began having a mirror fest with herself, appreciating her body on a daily basis, and eventually, she learned to love the whole package, breasts included. Once she rewrote her body script in this way, having bigger breasts was no longer important to her.

Uncovering the Total Woman (the Goddess) Inside You

Once you practice the mirror fest exercise, drink yourself in, and even more importantly, believe it, and this new love for yourself begins to permeate your essence and you reflect it to the outer world. Have you ever noticed a woman who isn't particularly attractive in the physical sense, but who has men pursuing her with a vengeance? I remember a girl like this in college. She had so much goddess essence, that she had men lining up to be with her.

Who is a goddess? A goddess is a woman who believes in her beauty and grace. She is powerful and feminine and sensual. She exudes mystery, like she's holding herself as the best-kept secret. She shares her playfulness with both women and men, because she knows life is too rich to give all her attention to men alone. She waits for men to approach her, because she knows what she's worth. She is comfortable being by herself and if she chooses to be with a man, it's one who can take in the totality of who she is.

If this seems like a fantasy, it isn't. I've seen women in all shapes and sizes who carry this goddess essence. In fact, that's the point—a goddess isn't one type. She can be as thin and lithe as a model or as round and curvaceous as an earth mother. *It is who she is that defines her, not what she looks like.*

IMAGINE THIS

Two women go into a local bar. Both are well groomed and attractively dressed, one about twenty to thirty pounds overweight, the other a petite hard body. The one who's overweight is laughing and drinking her beer, having a great time. She's up dancing and the guys are lining up to be with her. Miss Hard Body is sitting by herself, clutching her Perrier at the bar. What's the difference between the two? The first woman believes she's a goddess—the second one doesn't.

Why is it important to practice goddess imaging? Because our body scripts have reinforced the opposite, namely, that we are trophies, sex objects, or sloppy seconds to the girls on *Baywatch*. It's hard for us to feel confident and strong in who we are when we are running these scripts on ourselves.

Fred Stemen has had excellent results with his subliminal *goddess tape* (see Resources Section) which helps women retrain their subconscious into believing they are both powerful and feminine. Fred puts these two messages together, because he wants to override the deep societal programming that little girls often get that they can be powerful but not feminine or feminine but not powerful. These erroneous beliefs get in the way of women appreciating who they are and cripple them in the areas of relationship and career.

In his tape, the goddess circles the sun or stars in a shimmery gown, comes back to earth, stands on a cliff high above others, and declares her identity and presence to all the creatures below who quake when they hear her voice. She is powerful, a force to be reckoned with, yet she is still soft and feminine. The final words on the tape are, "I am free," and she does feel free from all the other messages that told her she was less than a woman.

If you listen to this tape one or two times a day, you will plant the freeing message that you are both powerful and feminine. Over time, this message will permeate your essence and change your life.

It's important to note, though, that you shouldn't tell the man in your life that you are doing this. I have made that fatal mistake on more than one occasion and either scare the man off or leave him thinking I'm a prima donna. Part of being the goddess is being mysterious, and if you tell him what you're doing, he won't understand it and may even try to control you or use it against you if he thinks you're not acting like a goddess.

Don't tell him you want him to peel the grapes for you or take you on that moonlit walk. Just listen to the tape, appreciate your body in the mirror, and be the goddess. Either he'll notice and be drawn to you, at which time you can decide what you want to do with him, or he will be uncomfortable around you (because he can't handle your full essence), in which case you say, "Next?" if you're single, and move on. Or you could be lucky like one of my girlfriends Leslie who had a man literally drop to his knees, massage her legs, and say, "You're such a goddess."

Many of the married women who have used this goddess tape find it gives them a fresh spin on their marriage as they become new and mysterious in their husbands' eyes. They find themselves smiling more, becoming softer and more feminine, more confident and powerful, more playful, flirtatious, and sensuous. They experience their husbands picking up on these visual cues and becoming more attentive to them.

One woman, after listening to the tape, decided to cut her hair and try a different look. She arranged for her husband to meet her at a local bar and pick her up as if she were a new woman in his life, and take her home. It added playfulness to their relationship, and her husband was definitely enthusiastic, as if he were having an affair with a new woman.

Experiencing a New Sense of Freedom

Once we rewrite our body scripts with beliefs and actions that empower us, we experience a new sense of freedom with ourselves and our mothers. We can no longer blame them for looking or feeling a certain way because we finally realize that we have the power to change the way we treat and care for our own bodies. We have no more excuses for staying their fat little girls or developing eating disorders to get their attention or taking drugs to get even with them. We now make decisions from a desire to love and nurture ourselves instead of from anger, frustration, and an underlying belief that we are not good enough.

Gone is the battle we wage with our bodies, the striving to be perfect centerfolds. In its place is the freedom to re-create ourselves in the images we want, to choose men who love us the way we are, to celebrate our femininity and power at the same time.

Last Shot At Miss America:

Living Your Dreams Instead of

Your Mother's

The first female U.S. Supreme Court Justice,

Sandra Day O'Connor, probably has a mother who said,

"I never liked black on you."

When Our Mothers Steal Our Dreams

I was at a writers' party when I met Patty, an aspiring fiction writer. We were having a great time, discussing our love of writing, our hopes and dreams, when Patty confided, "I told my mother I was going to a writers' group and she said, 'You certainly go to a lot of writers' groups. Do *all* writers need that much criticism?'"

Patty was laughing, but I could tell that she was hurt, that in a few short words, her mother had tried to steal her dream. Patty has been waiting to publish her first book, a monumental task in and of itself. She didn't need her mother killing her hopes before she even got started.

When I asked Patty if she thought her mother was joking, she said no, that she had confronted her about the comment and she was quite serious. She added that she had seen her mother do the same thing to her father, undermine his dreaming side by insisting that he not have any dreams.

Nothing can tie up our date with destiny more than competing with our mothers who want to steal our dreams because they never lived their own, or mothers who try to live their dreams through us for the same reason. It keeps us stuck making decisions in reaction to them rather than setting our own goals. It causes us to put our own lives on hold by sidelining our dreams because we are afraid to leave our mothers behind. And when we do have those wins, it may even rob us of feeling good about them, because we somehow feel guilty that we won them at our mothers' expense.

DRAMA TRAP: PUTTING YOUR LIFE ON HOLD

When you get caught in the drama of competing with your mother, you may find yourself putting your life on hold by sidelining your own dreams. You may feel hesitant about going for your own wins and stay back with her to avoid conflict.

What is putting our lives on hold? It's not knowing what we want, not even giving ourselves permission to dream it in the first place. It's allowing ourselves to live in drama, which is uncomfortable, but familiar, instead of using our gifts and talents to make a difference in the world. It's hiding out in the life our mothers think is best for us, instead of risking a new life of our own making. It's lying to ourselves that our dreams aren't all that important compared to someone else's.

It starts with our mothers getting mad at us because we dare to grow up and leave them to create our own lives. When this happens, we remind them of their lost beauty, their lost youth, which they can never reclaim. This triggers their emotions in such a way that they begin to wonder what other dreams they left on the table—the trips they wanted to take but couldn't afford, the men they truly loved but never married, the careers they sacrificed to raise us. Their feelings become a mixture of fear and longing: fear that we are passing them by with our lives and a longing that we not miss some of the opportunities they did.

They want so badly for us to have everything they didn't have, but at the same time, they may become angry or jealous when we come close to having it, because it reminds them of what they wanted and thought they could never have.

That's when they may try sabotaging our success by becoming overly critical or controlling or when they may become more competitive with us to keep themselves in the game. Or they may become sarcastic like Patty's mother did, which is their way of slowing us down. Regardless of the way they do it, the underlying message is the same—"Don't pass me by. Stay back with me where I can feel I'm still in the game with you."

Because we may feel that our lives aren't our own, that our mothers are driving our destiny, we may feel more compelled than ever to compete with them. We may never have intended to do this, but we are feeling so out of control with our own lives that competing back makes us feel in control of something, so we go after our mothers.

MAMA DRAMA MINUTE

I never realized the effect my bragging had on my mother. I used to call her up and tell her how beautiful California was, about my trips, my clothes, my dinners, my house that looked like it was designed by Frank Lloyd Wright. One time, I got carried away, and said, "My Jacuzzi is so big, you can fit twenty people in it." She quickly shot back, "There aren't twenty people in California I'd want to get into a Jacuzzi with." Her sarcasm was her way of letting me know I wasn't such a hot shot after all.

Years later, when she divorced and remarried a wealthy man, it was payback time, her turn to flash the diamond ring and fur coat. This competition definitely got in the way of the relationship we could have had all along.

We must be honest with ourselves about the ways we feed the competition. We brag; we announce every personal victory; we even criticize our mothers and then we wonder why they're so mad at us, why they can't be more supportive of our dreams. The very fact that we feel a need to compete with them in these ways is a sign that we are not feeling good about ourselves. If we truly felt the strength of our power and the satisfaction of our accomplishments, there would be no need to keep the competition going.

Our mothers' intrusion into our lives can be even worse when they want to live vicariously through us. They don't just want to compete with us—they want to have second lives through us. They don't just expect us to be or act a certain way—they expect us to make up for their disappointments and lost dreams. It's their last shot at being Miss America, and this time, they're determined not to blow it.

They may become so attached to an outcome with us that they becomes martyrs and put their own lives on hold just to make sure that we fulfill our dreams. They may do this joyfully, like women on a mission, or with great suffering, like they're sacrificing everything for us and we had darn well better appreciate it.

The mothers who epitomize this dynamic are the stage mothers and mothers of cheerleaders, who never made it themselves but start riding their daughters early in childhood to be star performers. They are so invested in their daughters' making it that they have no room for letting their girls learn from their own mistakes and choose their own destinies.

They fail to see how their zealousness is anything but encouraging; in reality, it is a setup for failure. The underlying message is that the outcome, not their daughters, is more important, and the daughters only feel validated when they get the outcome their mothers want. It's a trap that keeps us grown-up daughters chasing our mothers' approval and the perfect outcome the rest of our lives. It's also a heavy burden to bear, one that most of us can't carry without rebelling at some point in our lives.

Barbara's Story: Living Mother's Lost Dreams

Barbara's mother was a performer, a child acrobat and dancer with the USO after World War I. She loved dancing, but had to give up her career in the theater because she couldn't dance without her thick eyeglasses, and there were no contacts available at the time. So she followed her mother's advice, got married, and had children of her own.

Barbara was the only girl in the family, and her mother, still frustrated from her own lost dreams, was more determined than ever to make her into the star she had never been. So she drove Barbara an hour each way to the city to get her dance, voice, and acting lessons.

When it came time for Barbara to enter the Junior Miss pageant, her mother insisted she do things her way, fighting for two weeks over which performance she should do. Barbara finished as a finalist, but didn't win, and she felt awful, like she had let her mother down.

Instead of comforting Barbara, her mother berated her: "If my mother had given me the chances I've given you, I'd be in Hollywood or on the stage now." Barbara was devastated. Her mother had been giving her double messages, one minute pressuring her to be the star, and the next telling her she wasn't really good enough to make it. All she could do was scream at her mother to leave her alone, to go be onstage, if it was so important to her. Then she'd go off with her dog and cry.

What she really needed at that moment was some comforting and nurturing, to know that she was somebody apart from her ability to perform. But Barbara never got that kind of validation from her mother, and she continued to find solace in her friends and pets, substitutes for the nurturing mother she wanted.

In spite of her mother's efforts to make her the star, Barbara never got her big break in the theater. She did summer stock when she was a kid, performed in high-school and college plays and community theater, but never went all the way with her career as a performer. It was almost as if her mother's need to compete with her and live through her robbed her of any real sense of accomplishment in this arena.

Both of her parents regarded her career as mere window dressing, telling her instead that her job was to be a nice Jewish girl and marry well. So, true to form, Barbara married well, became the wife of a doctor as her mother had done before her. She thought this was what she wanted, but soon she discovered the relationship was just another disappointment. "I married a man who had a switchblade for a tongue," Barbara explained. "He was my mother, my father, my brother, and everyone else who had become the heavy critic in my life."

Over the years, the marriage became so verbally abusive she couldn't tolerate it anymore and when it started to become physically abusive, she decided to leave. Her mother was less than understanding, telling her daughter that she was nuts for leaving her husband and asking her how she was going to take care of herself and her daughters. But Barbara told her she had to leave for her own sanity and physical well-being.

Suddenly, marrying well was a failed game plan for her life, and she struggled. She tried a variety of jobs, but nothing seemed to click. Barbara had gone from being somebody's daughter to somebody's wife to somebody's mother and lost herself more with each role. Nobody bet on her talents, including herself. Her mother continued to tell her she was a screwup, her ex-husband portrayed her as a failure, and her own daughters bought into these messages.

"When I moved away from being the nice Jewish girl and had both financial and health setbacks, I was forced to reexamine my life. I asked, 'Who am I? What am I really made of? Why am I still here?'" As hard as it was for her to let go of her husband and face being on her own, it forced her to reset her priorities, to ask, for the first time in her life, what she wanted.

She realized forgiving her mother was essential to getting what she wanted. "I came face-to-face with the fact that in order to get on with my life, and embrace self-love as well as create room for any other loving relationships, I had to forgive her. Forgiving is not forgetting. My mother loves me in the way she's capable of loving, which can be superficial. She doesn't know unconditional love—there are always strings attached."

So how did Barbara learn to live with the strings attached?—by detaching from the drama and competition. When her mother tried to engage her, she'd make a joke or change the subject. She learned to give her mother the spotlight and find her own spotlight elsewhere. And she focused on creating her dreams so she wouldn't pass on her mother's sense of frustration to her daughters.

These moves have led her to the work she loves, coaching speakers from her theatrical and voice backgrounds, to a more honest and loving relationship with her own daughters, and to a relationship with a man who adores her the way she is. Her destiny is finally clicking, and she feels more hopeful than ever about her future.

Filtering Through Our Mothers' Agendas

Listening to Barbara's story, I couldn't help but think, "Now this was a mother with an agenda for her daughter." First her mother wanted her to be the star, to make up for the theatrical career she lost. Then her mother wanted her to marry well when, like her, dreams of a real career weren't possible. Then, when the marriage failed, her mother wanted her to stay in the relationship, for financial security and appearances, which is exactly what her mother did in her marriage. Her mother was directing her life, and Barbara was allowing it, until she decided to take some risks and go out on her own.

In our new beliefs about our mothers we learned that our mother's primary agenda is wanting "the good life" for us. If we want to get more details about what that good life is, we need to get closer to her and her dreams.

TRY THIS

Interview your mother on videotape or just get her talking around the family photo album. You will discover some of her hidden dreams and stories, and these will reflect her wishes for you. Listen for key themes, for reasons why she made certain choices or for excuses why she didn't do something. Also look for clues in her demeanor, dress, and environment. These indicators will give you insights into her values and fears, which may be influencing your life choices.

We have to remember that our mothers don't have a plan to ruin our lives, no matter how much it may seem that way. There's nothing wrong with marrying well or any other strategy our mothers may suggest, as long as we realize it's not the only strategy, and as long as it's something we want as well. Our job isn't to try to destroy our mothers' agendas, but rather to understand them and go about the business of living our own dreams.

Diane's Story: Putting Her Life on Hold to Work for Her Mother

"I always joked that I started working for my mother as soon as I learned the alphabet," Diane said. "I remember filing supplements for her law books when I was just a young girl." Diane started putting in serious hours for her mother when she was in junior high and high school. When she was eighteen, her sisters were sure she was going to move out, but she stayed and went to work for her mother full-time in her law practice. She gave up trying to go to college, because it was too much to do both.

"I'd dread going into work," she confessed. "I didn't know what kind of a mood my mother was going to be in, if I was going to be the angel who could do no wrong or the bitch who could do no right." Her mother was a tough taskmaster, heavy on the work and light on the praise. Almost every four years, she'd fire Diane because she was dissatisfied with her work. Then a few weeks later, she'd beg Diane to come back and just watch the phones, which always turned into Diane going back to work for her.

On one level, Diane was relieved to go back, because it was better than the crummy jobs she worked when she left her mother. But it was also painful working for a mother who didn't appreciate her.

Her mother would often hire people for more money, people who cheated her and didn't do the same quality work Diane did, and when Diane confronted her about this, her mother was quick to explain why they were worth more. This did nothing but undermine Diane's confidence in herself, but she still stayed, because her job with her mother was better than the other jobs she could get without a college education. Things would be fine for a while until her mother would fire Diane again and the cycle would start over.

This pattern of getting fired and going back to work for her mother was very damaging for Diane. She felt temporary relief having her job back and being in familiar conflict with her mother, compared to the unknown of finding another job. But this really wasn't relief for her, because each time she went back, her self-esteem shrunk a little more.

One day, Diane finally reached her breaking point and decided to leave her mother's office. She gave her mother six weeks' notice and made plans to go to broadcasting school. After Diane left, her mother told her she never realized how much work she did, but the damage had already been done. "There was the intellectual part of me that said, 'You're wonderful, intelligent, and powerful,' and then there was the voice inside of me that said, 'No you aren't. Just shut up and do your work. This is all you deserve.' " She had a tough time getting past that voice, the voice of her mother's critic that was still telling her she was unworthy of a better life.

After broadcasting school she accepted a job at a local radio station, but once again found herself in the position of working long hours for low pay. When her station was bought out by a larger company, she offered to stay on and do more, hoping that things would change, but of course they never did. At the time, she was still listening to that voice that told her she didn't deserve anything, let alone more. That voice kept her overweight, kept her in relationships with men who mistreated her, and kept her in her mother's professional shadow.

By the time Diane found her mentor, a personal success coach, she had finally reached the point where she was ready to make some radical changes in her life and find her own blueprint for success. Up to this time she had made her destiny more by reacting to her mother (what her mother needed, what her mother told her) than by paying attention to her own desires and talents.

Her mentor gave her subliminal tapes to help her boost her self-esteem and refocused her on what she wanted in her life, giving her a sense of purpose and self-worth. He identified her old pattern of putting up with a crummy job (because that's all she felt she deserved) and challenged her to take new action outside of this pattern to find a better job in broadcasting, for this was truly her career love.

Once Diane changed jobs, she felt so empowered by her action that her attitude changed across the board, and she found other areas of her life improving. She was able to work for her mother on a part-time basis, this time on her terms, for more money and fewer hours. She began to lose weight. She was able to see her future (career, relationships) with more hope and promise. And her relationship with her mother also improved dramatically once she took her own life off hold and began to develop her own professional identity.

Finding Your Own Blueprint for Success

You may be doing the same thing as Diane, using your mother's life and your mother's career to put your own life on hold, when in fact you need to carve out your own professional identity. Or you may have bought into her criticism and excuses to the point where you've become very skilled at making your own excuses. You may even believe that you're helpless or incompetent, which simply isn't true.

The only way to deal with these excuses is to challenge them with new beliefs, speak your intentions, then act on your intentions one at a time. For this to work you have to have an appetite for the life you want. You have to ask boldly for what you want and expect that you will get it.

This method counters the way many of us were raised as little girls. We were told to be more realistic or accommodating in our goals. We were told that other people would take care of us. We were told that we couldn't have it all, that sacrifices would have to be made. We can have it all, all that's important to us, one piece at a time. It will require some planning, some choosing, some juggling, but we can have it.

I have a friend who is a master negotiator, and he told me that the "what" is more important than the "how," that once we know what we want, the how will reveal itself to us. It can come to us in the most unexpected ways, through other people, through our reading, through a fortunate set of circumstances. Once we lock on to what we want with full desire, we will find the steps to reach our goal.

TRY THIS

Have you ever noticed how people save up their dreams to live tomorrow? It's one of the ways we hide behind our fear of going for what we want. The solution to putting your life on hold is to start living your dreams today in small ways. For example, you may have a goal of owning a house on the ocean, but can't afford it right now. You could start living your dream by taking walks on the beach or renting a vacation home on the ocean.

Once you start giving yourself even small pieces of your dreams, it will be easier for you to see your dream and move confidently toward achieving it.

As women, we are used to nurturing others so we may not make ourselves a priority, let alone give ourselves permission to ask what we want. Yet we cannot hit a target in our career or life until we know what that target is, so asking what we want becomes all the more important. Finding our own blueprint for success is keeping our focus on what we want until we get it. It sounds simple, but it is actually more challenging for women because we are used to dissipating our focus on the people we nurture, on the multiple tasks we juggle in the course of any given day. To learn how to have singular focus, we must become the huntress.

Becoming the Huntress: Developing Your Ability to Zero In on Your Goals

A mercenary is someone who is motivated solely for money or gain. Most of us cringe at the word, because we see pictures of soldiers for hire on devious missions. But there is something we can learn from the mercenary, namely, that he doesn't deviate from his purpose of completing the mission and benefiting himself in the process. As women going for our dreams we need to learn this very important strategy, so that the only plan for our lives isn't being the good daughter and marrying well.

My mentor told me when I was plotting my new career as a speaker/author that I must become a *financial mercenary on my own behalf.* He said that I must have a singular focus on my mission, namely to get this book published and launch my career, and that nothing could distract me from that purpose.

TRY THIS

Many women find it helpful to have a mentor or a group of mentors in the form of a mastermind group or Princessa Roundtable (see Resources Section). Mentors help keep you focused on your goals and wins and coach you in how to move through any obstacles and setbacks you may experience. Form a small group of four or five women who are like-spirited and committed to reaching their goals and serve as mentors for each other.

He explained that men already have singular focus, the ability to zero in on the task at hand—if they're making the sale, that is their focus. If they're trying to bed a woman, they're equally determined. He told me this instinct in men was primal, that it dated back to caveman days when the man's job was to go outside the cave and hunt for food. If the man didn't have a singular focus, his family would starve and die.

Cavewomen, on the other hand, had multiple focus. They stayed in the cave, tended the fire, cooked the meals, watched the children, tanned the hides, juggled several tasks at once.

This multiple focus is a great asset until we allow it to distract us from our goals. For example, there's a single mother who's already juggling one or two major projects at work that are essential to her financial future, her kids before and after work, and a board position on the PTA. All of a sudden, Mr. Right comes into her life and she wants to spend time with him, so she starts juggling some more, only to discover that one of her projects starts to suffer or the kids are getting cranky because she's too exhausted and scattered to keep up.

Why did this happen for the woman and not the man? Quite frankly because the man was able to compartmentalize his life. When he went off to work, he didn't think about her or the candlelit dinner she just cooked for him. He was on the hunt for another deal. When he wants her again, he'll put his attention on her and not a second sooner.

The woman became distracted. Instead of focusing on closing her sale, she was wondering what her man really thought of the dinner last night, if this meant the two of them were becoming closer, if he would be open to more commitment in the relationship. With her multiple focus, she was running a whole scenario that interfered with her ability to have a singular focus on her sale.

For the most part, our differing strengths in singular and multiple focuses complement one another, but once a woman wants to take charge of her career and destiny, she must be able to develop a singular focus like her male counterpart, so she is not distracted and pulled off course.

There is also a difference in our power bases, in the ways we derive and extend our power. Men draw their sense of power, security, and self-worth from their work, the hunt, and bring that back to their cave, the home. Women draw the same sense of power, security, and self-worth from their home, the cave, and then extend it outwardly to the world, the hunt. A woman's cave includes her relationships with all her extended family and friends. It is her sanctuary, her sacred space in which she nurtures those she loves and spins her own dreams.

If a man's outer world is in chaos and turmoil, he will bring that into his home and his relationships. And if a woman's relationships are in trouble, she will find it difficult to be productive in the outer world.

MOTIVATION TO HEAL THE MAMA DRAMA

Once we understand that when our relationships are in trouble, we will find it difficult to be productive in the outer world, and so we should be more motivated than ever to heal our mama drama. We may think we can handle it, but until we resolve it, we will wear our conflict with our mothers in everything we do.

When we become serious about going for our goals, we must have harmony in our cave and relationships in order to be productive in the outer world. We must be willing to follow the scent of the hunt, even when it leads us away from the familiar paths our mothers gave us. We must forage for opportunities, take our scrapes and wounds with destiny, retreat to our caves, and go out again the next day after bigger game. We must be willing to risk leaving our loved ones (our children, husbands) long enough to go for our own wins, knowing that we will return to love them again and draw our strength from the cave once more.

We are used to the hunt when it comes to marrying well—we aren't afraid to go to any length to snare our man. Why then won't we do it with our own destiny? Perhaps because we're afraid we'll get lost in the hunt and leave our feminine qualities behind. Not so—we will emerge from the hunt as goddesses, more feminine than ever and stronger for being in the hunt.

The first time I experienced being the huntress, I was so hungry and aroused when I returned home, all I wanted to do was to have sex and eat a steak. I was finally tapping into my primal power, and it was exhilarating! Suddenly, I understood why men love to cut loose after the hunt. That night I went to a summer party and when I was there, I was drawing men to me so furiously, I almost didn't know what to do with them. At one point I had five different men massaging me on my legs, arms, and back of my neck, others getting me drinks, and others asking me out. My femininity did not suffer by being in the hunt.

The mistake we make in living our destiny is settling for the cave when we want the hunt, or thinking we have to choose between the cave and the hunt when we want them both. There is nothing wrong with the cave. We need it. But we also need the hunt, to know what it feels like to test our strengths in the wilderness of the unknown.

Developing Your Ability to Have a Singular Focus

Before we can develop our ability to have a singular focus, we must understand something about the information we are juggling. Hypnotherapy teaches us that at any given time our minds can only handle three to seven "chunks" of reality, meaning no more than three to seven things at a time (compared to the fifteen to twenty chunks most of us try to juggle). A chunk of reality is anything we perceive, consciously or unconsciously, at any given moment. These chunks of reality have different levels of complexity.

For example, if I asked you to walk on a 2´-by-4´ board lying on the ground, this would be considered one chunk of reality, and a simple one at that, because there is no risk to you if you fall off the board. It is so simple, you could probably do it blindfolded or do it backward. You could even handle other tasks (or chunks) with it, such as chewing gum, reading the newspaper, listening to music.

But if I stretched that same 2´-by-4´ board between two forty-story office buildings and asked you to walk across it, the complexity of this chunk of reality would change drastically. All of a sudden your risk level would skyrocket, because the consequences of your falling could mean your very life. Given this situation, you could not handle anything else but the task of getting across that board.

The same concept, that *it is the complexity of the chunk, not just the number of chunks*, affects our ability to have a singular focus. We think we can handle more, but we can't. We especially can't when we're already dealing with complex chunks. At certain times, like when we're driving, it's very dangerous to try to handle more chunks. Scanning our fifteen to twenty chunks can actually cause us to go into a trancelike state and not see things. That's when we run through red lights without even seeing them and get in accidents.

I had this happen to me after my last divorce. My complex chunks were: the divorce, my kids, the book, and speaking. Anything I tried to add in only complicated my life. Suddenly, after twenty-seven years of a near-perfect driving record, I had three accidents in six months because I was trying to juggle too many chunks while I was driving. I actually went to a hynotherapist who explained this chunk concept to me and had me do a brain dump on a notepad every time I got in the car. Once I got the fifteen to twenty things out of my head, I was free to have a singular focus on my driving. It has worked beautifully, and I have been accident-free ever since.

TRY THIS

Just assigning your chunks to paper (or a pocket tape recorder) will free you up to have a singular focus.

- Try doing your own brain dump before you drive, before you visit your mother, before you make a special presentation or start a new project. You can simply write the chunks down on a notepad or use one of the many excellent time-management systems, which allows you to compartmentalize these chunks into such areas as daily tasks, finances, and projects.

Stephen R. Covey, author of *The 7 Habits of Highly Effective People,* has developed The 7 Habits Organizer, which encourages users to organize their tasks by their roles (mother, wife, writer, etc.) and goals, and identify how much time they are spending in each role for greater balance in their lives (see Resources Section).

- Assign all tasks to a schedule.

Use the color block method of scheduling, using different colors for different blocks of time (for example, purple for appointments, red for kids, green for financial, pink for creative projects). This will give you a quick visual cue that you're now working in a creative block of time or moving to a kid block of time, and helps you shift your focus from one type of time to another. It also reassures you, on the subconscious level, that you are exactly where you are supposed to be.

Once you assign everything to a schedule (or place in your time-management system), it immediately gives your subconscious the message that a chunk is handled for the time being and will be completed in the future, and this can relieve your anxiety.

- Use your voice mail, answering machine, or headphones (with your favorite music) to block out distractions and interruptions while you're working on creative projects.

Another concept that helps tremendously in developing a singular focus is *pacing and shifting tasks to complete them in their best time.* Even when you get your chunks down to a more manageable three to seven, it's still easy to get overwhelmed by the complexity of certain chunks. This is when it becomes important to pay attention to when you have the best energy level to do certain types of work. For example, you may find that your best time to do financial, organizational, and administrative tasks is early morning, followed by doing your creative tasks midmorning and midafternoon, and correspondence at the end of the day.

TRY THIS

If you find yourself getting overwhelmed by all your tasks, picture an imaginary line from your nose going out into infinity, with your tasks strung along that line. Touch your nose with your index finger and say, "Silly me, I'm doing it again. What can I do next?" or "What do can I actually do now?" This technique is a pattern interrupt, an alternative to worrying about your tasks, as well as a physical cue to literally do what's right in front of your nose. One attorney trained herself and her staff to do this and noticed a dramatic increase in productivity in her office. All day long she and her coworkers can be seen touching their noses to remind them to stay focused on the task at hand.

You may find yourself so overwhelmed by your workload that you need to take breaks to refresh and refocus yourself. My friend Ariela Wilcox taught me a technique called *mistuveving* when she was helping me shape the first drafts of this book. *Mistuveve* is a Hebrew word which means to mill or wander around in a semifocused way, such as window-shopping, browsing in a bookstore, or walking through a street fair. It is a glorious activity that gives your brain a much-needed rest, while still recharging your creativity. I included going to the movies in my mistuveving and used this technique to help overcome any writer's block I experienced while writing this book. The physical movement and browsing helped me get unstuck and feel less overwhelmed with my work.

Sometimes the best way you can regain your focus is by shifting certain tasks to another time altogether, when you'll be more up to it. This requires that you are honest with yourself about what you can and can't handle, that you slow down and match your tasks to a more natural rhythm. One woman I know suffers from such bad PMS for two weeks that she marks this as the red zone in her calendar. During this time, she scales back, asks her husband to cook more, takes more time to pamper herself, does more quiet, creative projects. She saves her most intense work for the blue zone, those two weeks when she isn't exhausted from PMS.

TRY THIS

Now that you understand you can only handle three to seven chunks of reality, depending on the complexity of the chunk, at any given time, use this understanding to shift projects and tasks.

---

1. TAKE AN HONEST ASSESSMENT OF YOUR CHUNKS.

You are the best barometer of how complex your chunks are. You know how much anxiety you're feeling, how much you can really handle. You have to be careful not to compare yourself with others who may appear to be handling more chunks than you. What works for them probably won't work for you.

This is a tough one because we currently live in a culture that tells us we're superwomen and should be able to handle everything at once. Even the best world-class jugglers know when to add in another object, so as not to upset the pattern. We, too, must learn this skill of pacing.

2. DON'T ADD TASKS WHEN YOU'RE HANDLING COMPLEX CHUNKS.

The week you're making a major sales presentation or the week your kids have their dance recital is not the week to take on extra projects. The time you are recovering from a divorce or rebuilding a career is not the best time to start a new relationship.

By the way, decisions are also considered chunks of reality and can be extremely stressful. It is most stressful making the decision, then implementing the decision, then waiting for the results. Be sure not to make your most important decisions when you're handling too many chunks but rather reschedule them for another time when you can give them your full attention and energy.

Expect Periods of Testing

In the transition from being someone's daughter to someone's wife to someone's mother, we may not have had much opportunity to test ourselves in the wilderness. We certainly didn't learn the hunt from our mothers. Most of them stayed in the cave, and those who did venture out did so in safe careers that never really gave them a sense of the hunt.

But once we make the decision to claim our destiny, we will find ourselves in the hunt, in a wilderness where we'll be tested at every turn in the journey. It is a curious mixture of fear and exhilaration. Each time, it will feel like we can't possibly survive, but we will. We'll put another pelt on our huntress's belt and follow the scent of the win all over again.

In aikido, we learn to expect periods of testing. Each practice is a test in and of itself, a test of being in the moment, a test of staying connected to our partners and moving with their energy, a test of emptying our minds of all the distractions that get in the way of our practice.

We also have periods of more formal testing when we experience *randori*, almost simultaneous attacks from multiple opponents. It forces us to stay clear and present and deal with each attack the only way we can deal with it, one at a time.

I remember the week I passed my first aikido test. As the sweat poured down my face and my muscles ached, I had no choice but to keep going. The more I focused, the smoother it became, until the very end when the techniques were no longer outside of me but part of me. It was exhausting and exhilarating and so rewarding to know I had finally passed.

When we attempt living our destinies, not our mothers', it can be just as exhilarating. It requires that we leave the familiar paths of competing with our mothers, putting our lives on hold or allowing them to live through us, and instead test ourselves on new challenges in the wilderness. It requires that we leave our caves, the safety of being our mothers' daughters, to find the wonder of who we truly are. And it requires that we follow the scent of our own wins, knowing full well that we will return to our cave and clan, and be stronger women for it.

What Being in the Hunt Does for Our Daughters

When my oldest daughter Meghan stood up in her Brownie ceremony and told the audience she wanted to be a writer, a speaker, an artist, a scientist, a professional basketball player, and a mommy, I was flabbergasted. I think when I was her age I wanted to be a mommy and a teacher, because teacher was one of two acceptable professions for women. I know I didn't have the scope of dreams she did. Call it pride, but I like to think that I've had some influence over my daughter seeing multiple dreams for herself, at least the writer and speaker parts—her dad can take credit for the professional basketball player.

Meghan was only six years old when I began writing my book, and she couldn't wait to write hers. She informed me she was writing a series of books, not just one, featuring a different animal for each month of the year, and the first book was called *The March Bunny*. One day she came back over to my house from her father's place, and informed me that she was an author, too, but that her book had already been published, unlike Mommy's book that was still waiting to be sold. Her father had hole-punched her book and tied it with pink ribbon and told her it was published and that was good enough for her.

I had to laugh at her exuberance, at her competitiveness with me, and I wondered just when they planted that competition gene in daughters anyway. I realized this was a critical moment, that I could fuss over her accomplishment, minimize it, or ignore it, that she was looking to me for some approval. I scooped her up in my arms, gave her a kiss, and gushed over her precious book.

Ever since that day, she has peeked her head in my office and given me updates, telling me about the latest book in her series, wondering if my agent will sell her book, too, wanting to know if she can sell her books with mine at the back of the room at my speaking engagements. As far as she's concerned, she's on a par with me and is just waiting for Oprah to call her. Now her younger sister Allison is joining our authors' circle by penning two of her own books, *Angels* and *Rosie the Rose*. If only they'll let Mommy manage their careers!

When we have the courage to go for our dreams, we give our daughters permission to do the same, to use our dreams as springboards for their own, to inspire them to be all that they can be. It is one of the most powerful ways that we change their lives, their destinies. We let them live in the world of what can be instead of what we missed and wished we'd done, and that is so freeing to both of us.

In seeing how many dreams my own mother left on the table, I became more determined than ever to live my own, because I didn't want to be a cranky old woman sitting in her rocking chair taking shots at my grown daughters for living their dreams. That's what I didn't want, and as motivating as it was, it wasn't the best motivation, because it was taking me away from the pain of unfulfilled dreams instead of toward the ecstasy of my own realized dreams.

Now I see my destiny as a series of shooting stars, with my daughters' stars right alongside me, and I'm already experiencing the joy that comes from sharing dreams together. It is just the beginning of my dreaming, of my daughters' dreaming—there is so much more out there.

Somewhere in your life there is an unrealized dream just waiting to be born. Please tap it for yourself and tap it for your children. It is part of the blessing, the precious legacy you give them.

The Power Illusion:

How to Stop Giving Your Power

Away to Your Mother

I'm forty-three years old, and my mother is still asking

me what I'm going to wear to dinner. At least this time,

she won't have to cut my meat for me.

Running Away from Our Mothers

Imagine a toddler who grabs her teddy bear and announces to her mother that she is running away from home. She makes a mad dash for the front door and, before she opens it, stops to see her mother smiling at her from the hallway. Gaining confidence, she takes a few steps down the sidewalk and stops again, to see her mother standing in the doorway. Feeling very bold, she starts her journey down the street, looking back every few steps to make sure her mother is still watching her. As soon as she turns the corner and can no longer see her mother, she begins to panic. She realizes cutting her mother off, grabbing the goods and running, isn't the solution. She needs to separate from her mother, to find and test the limits of her own capabilities, but this isn't the way to do it. She runs back to a smiling mother who never let her out of her sight and welcomes her back with open arms.

Like the toddler, we, too, want to run away from our mothers. And we, too, are just as conflicted. We want so desperately to separate from them, to become ourselves, but we are terrified of what this will mean in our lives. What if our mothers don't love us anymore? What if our mothers won't let us come back? What if we can't make it on our own?

DRAMA TRAP: BEING AFRAID TO LEAVE YOUR MOTHER

You compromise your power when you're afraid to separate from your mother for fear of losing her love or approval.

As long as we are desperate for our mothers' love and approval, as long as these things matter more to us more than what we think of ourselves, we will be under our mothers' control. To truly turn the corner in our relationship, we must be willing to leave them, to carve out our own identities, and to reunite with them on different terms. If we do this well, we will be able to be ourselves around them. If we do it poorly, we will be struggling to find ourselves in the drama.

Disengaging from our mothers may be a bit tricky. Why?—because they are just as conflicted as we are. If they accept us as separate from them, they have to confront their own anxiety. What if we don't need them or love them anymore? What if we go away and never come back? Even though they know we need to leave, they won't like our new moves with them and may do everything in their power to keep things the way they were, because it will make them feel more in control. And, just like the mother of the toddler, they'll be watching, waiting to take us back if the going gets too tough.

What they don't realize is that if they impede this process of leaving, their job of relating to us will be much tougher because we'll always be dependent on them. If they encourage us in the process, we will actually be drawn back to them, because we will feel so comfortable with ourselves we will want to share our lives with them.

Until we leave our mothers, we will spend a large part of our lives trying to be nothing like them, which is merely an act of rebellion. Eventually, we will get older and realize that we are a lot like them, and wish we'd accepted it sooner, because denying it only kept us in the struggle longer. The truth is we are our mothers' daughters, but we are not our mothers. Once we're at peace with this, our relationship can truly change.

MAMA DRAMA MINUTE

For most of my adult life, I either tried to be just like my mother or I rejected her completely. Either way I was still under her control, locked in an eternal power struggle that never seemed to go away.

In my twenties, I was the perfect clone. I had the same short hairdo and wore the same baggy, sexless clothes. I liked the same foods, talked the same politics, went to the same doctors, enjoyed the same things my mother enjoyed.

In my thirties I got married, moved to California, and totally rebelled against her. I permed my already naturally curly hair, wore a leopardskin bikini, and used way too much pink eye shadow. I stopped eating red meat, went to juice bars, and started seeing alternative-medicine doctors. I ran from everything she held sacred and chased other things I should have left alone.

In spite of my best efforts to carve out my own identity, I was utterly lost, stuck in this dance of emulating or rejecting her. The more I resisted her, the stronger the pull to be like her. Eventually, I'd just snap back, be my old self, and fight with her some more. I was so busy reacting to her, jumping from drama to drama, that I couldn't hear the underlying rumblings of what I needed as a woman.

My mother got more and more frustrated with me. She saw my wanderings as pure mutiny and tried to control me even more, to get me to be the good, compliant daughter she wanted.

Why We Give Our Power Away
to Our Mothers

Why are we so inclined to give our power away to our mothers in the first place? The reasons are endless: because we think we're supposed to be good, compliant daughters and not buck the system; because we don't think we really have a choice in the matter; because we've been doing it so long in our families; because we don't completely understand what we're doing; because we want to avoid confronting our mothers; because we want to avoid risking our mothers' love.

Many of us were raised in traditional families, where power—the ability to express ourselves as autonomous individuals—was discouraged. We were supposed to do what was good for the family, not good for ourselves, and anytime we questioned the family system, including our mothers, it was considered an act of rebellion.

Our mothers themselves may not have modeled true power for us. They might have taken subordinate roles in our families and taught us more about submitting to others than holding our own. They might have felt so powerless in their own careers or relationships that they couldn't be themselves with us and instead spent much of their time in drama, depression, or neediness. If we grew up with these examples, we wouldn't even know there was another way to be. Unless we had one of those rare, independent mothers who encouraged us to be fearless in our own ways, we may never have learned to flex our power muscles.

For some of us, the feminist movement of the sixties and seventies came into play, as it propelled us into a series of rebellions which made us feel powerful, but only alienated our mothers further. Suddenly we had choices our mothers never had, and felt we had to challenge their every belief and move. None of us knew how to handle this new, emerging power. Our efforts to separate and create our own identities in some ways became more complicated, as we mirrored the birthing pains of a generation that was breaking free not only from their mothers, but from the male establishment as well.

The Illusion of False Power—What It Looks Like When We Give Our Power Away to Our Mothers

If we were raised by domineering mothers, we may fall into the trap of living the extremes, caving in to them, or trying to overpower them just so we can have some sense of ourselves. Either way we are still under their control, because everything we are doing is in reaction to them. Even if we do feel we've defeated them in some way and that makes us feel powerful for a moment, it won't last. It is nothing more than *false power,* the illusion of being separate and in control based on actions designed by us to get back at our mothers.

This false power shows up in a number of ways:

- We become more reactive to our mothers.
- We rebel against them.
- We procrastinate.
- We avoid telling them the truth.
- We stay mad at them.
- We blame them for everything.

We feel like we're in control, but we aren't, because we are still letting our mothers' comments and actions drive us. We think we're being ourselves, but we're not, because we're too busy trying to second-guess our mothers. When we use these false-power moves, we are more trapped than ever in our powerlessness.

Reacting

A host of a radio talk show was interviewing me when she confessed that she kept her own apartment quite messy in reaction to her mother being a neat freak. "I knew that my mother was uncomfortable in a messy house, and therefore she would never come over to my house because it was always a mess."

"So that was your way of protecting your space," I commented, and she agreed: "Exactly, my space was a mess, but it was my space. The house is clean now, which is a good thing, but for the longest time, I would think, 'This is crazy—just do the dishes.' "

Not cleaning her apartment was her way of avoiding conflict with her mother, her way of keeping her mother out of her space. But instead of feeling in control of her environment, she felt more trapped than ever because she didn't like living in a messy apartment. When this woman moved farther away from her mother and there was no longer the threat of her mother dropping in, she found it easier to clean her apartment. Why?—because she stopped reacting to her mother.

Whenever we do something to get to our mothers, consciously or unconsciously, we are reacting to them, and this can make us feel powerless and guilty. There is nothing wrong with a particular action as long as we understand why we are doing it and as long as it's something that serves us. If housekeeping isn't important to us, that's one thing. But if it isn't important to us because it bugs our mothers, we should probably take another look at it.

Rebelling

When Robin was growing up, there were certain things, such as perfect table manners, that her mother valued, and Robin's reaction was to resist doing them, "to go on strike" as her therapist later called it. "I often did the opposite of what my mother wanted me to do, to send her the message that she couldn't control me and didn't own me. I wanted her to know that if I did something, I'd do it on my terms," Robin said.

But Robin didn't stop there. She went so far as to create a whole new persona. "My sister was very beautiful and feminine, a good dresser, artistic, and I chose to be just the opposite of her. I didn't really care about my looks. I dressed down. I was the athletic tomboy."

She thought she was becoming her own person, but she was creating a false self that left little room for her femininity and creativity. It would take her years to embrace these aspects of herself, to see herself as the feminine, sensuous poet and writer she is today.

As teenagers we may think our rebellions are fairly harmless, and the truth is, many of them are. But if we lock into certain rebellions at this age and let them define us, we could spend years struggling to find our true power. That's why so many of us are late power bloomers—we never fully separated from our mothers and our first attempts at leaving were rebellions that took us further away from who we wanted to be. As long as we keep chasing our false self in reaction to our mothers, we will never find the authentic self we need to hold our power around our mothers.

Procrastinating

Procrastination is another avoidance tactic. When we procrastinate, we avoid telling our mothers something, and we protect ourselves from the ultimate confrontation. It is another move which takes us into false power, because it gives us the illusion that we're in control, when in fact we're at the mercy of the consequences that occur when we wait too long. We wrongly think that something will magically happen to rescue us from the situation.

When Erin was nineteen and home for the summer from college, her mother suggested that they go on a backpacking trip together. Erin didn't want to go, but she said yes just to pacify her mother. About ten days before they were supposed to leave, her mother was talking excitedly about the trip, and Erin realized she really didn't want to go and finally told her the truth. Her mother was crushed, devastated, because she had put so much planning and emotion into the trip. Erin realized later that putting off her true feelings had created more pain than giving her mother a simple no in the first place. It took months for her mother to forgive her.

We can forgive ourselves for being clueless about such moves when we're teenagers, but many of us do the same thing as grown women—we put off confronting our mothers so long that our indecision becomes our decision. Then we wonder why our mothers are so upset with us.

Until we can take our power back, become more proactive, and actually set aside a time to approach our mothers, we will always be at the mercy of our reactivity. And if we're not careful, a small problem can snowball into a much larger one.

Avoiding the Truth

Sometimes avoiding our mothers can be such a pattern in our lives that it goes underground and creates major breakdowns in our lives. Susan went to a therapist thinking her problem was sugar addiction, but her therapist showed her that it was her underlying pattern of giving in to her mother's demands and not expressing her own feelings that was causing her major stress. Susan's inability to confront her mother transferred to an inability to confront her boss and coworkers, so instead of being honest about her limits, she took on more and more work in an effort to appease them. This strategy caught up with her when she had trouble functioning at work—stomach problems, verbal and emotional outbursts, disorientation while driving. Eventually she had to go out on a stress leave to recuperate.

Susan was finally in a situation where she could no longer avoid confronting her mother. She told her mother the truth about her stress leave and refused her mother's offer to come and help. This was a big move for Susan and the start of her taking her power back. In small baby steps, coached by her therapist, she learned to say no to her mother more often, to explain less, to tell the truth more. Gradually, she learned to drop the need for her mother's approval as well as her quest for perfectionism, and her life became easier.

To hold our personal power with our mothers, we must be willing to tell them the truth, to say no, and risk their love and approval. This does not mean we have to bare our souls about everything, or purposely tell them something that may hurt them, but it does mean that we own what is true for us and deal with the consequences.

Staying Mad

When we stay mad at our mothers, we are demonstrating to them and to ourselves that they have power over our emotions. We are allowing our conflict with them or our anger at each other to define our relationship. We are attaching more to the drama, because it gives us an excuse for not claiming our power around them.

Refusing to forgive our mothers is actually another stalling tactic to avoid the reconciliation, because we feel we'll lose ground with them in our relationship. The truth is we lose more ground by waiting because every day the emotions go unresolved, the conflict festers into an open sore that drains both of us. We put stress on our bodies. We miss opportunities to share the good life with each other. We leave things unsaid, hugs ungiven, love unexpressed.

In the worst case scenario, we never forgive our mothers. We stay mad at them the rest of their lives, and they die before we forgive them. In a better scenario, we have a cooling-off period and move more quickly to make our peace with them.

There is nothing wrong with a time out if we use the silence productively, if we reflect on our part in the conflict and decide to let go. But if we let the anger go on unresolved, we are allowing ourselves to become victims, and we will never find our power that way.

We don't have to stuff our feelings to hold our power with our mothers, but we do have to get over them. We can cry and wail and do whatever we need to express them, but at a certain point, if we want our relationship back, we have to stop and make a decision to connect with our mothers again.

Blaming

Blaming our mothers is the ultimate trap of giving our power away, because we buy into the false belief that everything in our lives is our mothers' fault and therefore outside of our control. We are so convinced that they are out to destroy us, we become immobilized, incapable of releasing our emotions and making new decisions to move our lives forward.

I once met a woman whose boyfriend had convinced her that her mother was to blame for everything and was ruining her life. This woman's mother had legitimate reasons for believing that her daughter's boyfriend was not a good influence on her grandson, and she had become involved in his custody proceedings in court. When the woman missed a court hearing and fled the state with her son, the court considered that she might have kidnapped her son and sent a federal marshal looking for her.

I sat with her one painful afternoon when she was immobilized with fear, not wanting to be arrested, not knowing how to reconcile with her mother, not knowing what to do with a boyfriend who was continuing to play her against her mother. One of her biggest stumbling blocks was how to get past the belief that her mother was out to get her. Once she could see that her mother did have her best interests at heart and that the drama she was currently in was largely of her own making, she was able to move very quickly to reconcile with her mother and do what was best for her son. She made the decision to leave her boyfriend and drive to her mother's home for help. Her mother was eager to help her resolve matters with the court and get a fresh start.

Had this woman continued to blame her mother, had she refused to act, she might have been arrested and lost custody of her son. Her crisis had forced her to stop blaming her mother and take more positive action for herself and her son.

When we stop blaming our mothers and start facing the consequences of our own actions we are so much freer to create the life we want, and we actually create the opportunity for our mothers to be freer, too, because they are no longer the object of our blame.

What Happens to Us When We Give Our Power Away

When we give our power away to our mothers, we die from hiding our true selves. We deny who we really are; we suppress parts of ourselves we'd like to express; and we play roles instead of being ourselves. We become passive mutes too afraid to speak up for what we want. We become victims, willing to accept less than we deserve. We become martyrs, attached to our suffering with our mothers.

We shrink who we are to please our mothers and get along. We are inconsistent in our actions, swayed by every comment our mothers make. We don't hear or trust our intuition, because we don't have a clear enough sense of ourselves apart from our mothers. And, we feel so powerless, we are incapable of making even the simplest decisions.

I remember that a college boyfriend made me a low-cut halter dress for my birthday and it looked great on me. He probably wanted to see me in something that showed my body instead of the baggy, sexless clothes I usually wore. My mother took one look and told me I couldn't wear it anymore, because I didn't have the proper lingerie and she didn't want me to go braless. Here I was, a young woman in my twenties, and I stopped wearing a dress that looked great on me to please my mother.

It never occurred to me that I had options. I could have worn the dress behind my mother's back, but then I'd just be rebelling. I could have found a bra to wear with the dress, but then I'd be complying with her demands. I could have continued wearing it as is, not because I wanted to defy her, but because it looked great on me and made me feel sexy. Only this last option was a true-power option, because it was consistent with who I was (a beautiful, sexual young woman) and what I wanted (to dress in a way to show my body).

The real issue here wasn't the halter dress, but the whole way I dressed to avoid confronting my mother. I thought if I wore the same baggy clothes and hid my body the way she hid hers, I wouldn't be a threat to her. It worked for a while, but there was no denying my sexuality, and eventually it came out in the form of rebellion (the permed hair, pink eye shadow, leopardskin bikini).

When we comply with our mothers' demands, our needs don't go away—they just go underground and they will resurface later in the form of rebellion and maybe even total anarchy in our lives. We may go clicking along for years and then one day, our spirit can't stand it any longer and we have to break free. That's why some of us have a delayed adolescence in our thirties.

But we already know that rebellion is just more false power, and we have to let it go. Chasing false power is a lot like the dog races, where the hounds are trained to chase a mechanical rabbit. It is the illusion of the rabbit being real that keeps the dogs running. If one of the dogs actually catches the rabbit, he can no longer race, because he now knows that the rabbit he's been chasing is fake and this isn't what he really wants.

If we continue to chase false power, it will never be satisfying to us, because we, too, know that it is fake, a poor imitation of the real thing. We must look, instead, to finding some new moves that will satisfy us, moves that will leave us feeling separate and equal with our mothers.

Techniques for Expressing Your True Power

True power is inside you—it is not found in anything you can do to your mother. It is the ability to make comments and actions consistent with who you are and what you want, and the willingness to accept the consequences. The more you take responsibility for your life, the more you know who you are and who you are not, and the easier it is for you to express your true power.

Is knowing who you are a function of age? Some might argue so, since so many women don't have a clear sense of themselves until their thirties and forties when they've had enough experiences and setbacks to form their own life wisdom. There is definite value in such insight, and yet, I believe you can know yourself sooner.

I've had many girlfriends who had a clear understanding of who they were at a very young age, and their way of defining themselves was taking actions consistent with their beliefs about themselves. The more they acted, the more they knew who they were. The more they knew who they were, the easier it was for them to be consistent in their actions. How did they know if something wasn't consistent with who they were? They felt it wasn't right—they trusted their intuition, made an adjustment, and went on believing in themselves.

They didn't always know at first what it felt like to express their true power, but over the course of taking action and tuning in to themselves to see if it felt right, they learned these new moves. I'm sure they made their fair share of mistakes, but they chose to move in the direction of what worked, and this strategy got them to their true power sooner.

TRY THIS

To find your true power, learn to move more from your intuition.

- Be consistent in your quieting practice (prayer, meditation, walks) so that ideas have a chance to bubble up inside you.
- Keep a pocket tape recorder or notebook in several locations: in your car, on your nightstand, at your desk.
- When an idea pops into your mind or you get a strong feeling about something, record it. This may come in the form of picture, a symbol, a person's name, a memory, a sense about someone or yourself.
- Allow some time to sit with the idea. Don't feel rushed to act.
- Take action on these ideas and feelings.

It may take a while to develop this sixth sense of moving from your intuition, but over time it will feel more and more comfortable to you as you see what results from trusting it. It is actually a more natural way of moving, one that is always with us but one we can overlook in our busyness.

Slowing Your Responses

When your mother pushes your buttons as only she can do, you may feel a need to give her an immediate response, and this dilutes your power with her. This first response is probably not the best response, because you've already allowed your mother to hook your emotions, and you cannot express your true power when your emotions are out of control.

The better strategy is to avoid responding at the moment or to delay your response until later. This will give you time to check in with your intuition, that part of you that knows who you are and what you want, before you get back to your mother.

TRY THIS

Suppose your mother comes to you and says, "Why can't you be more like your sister?" This question puts you on the spot and could trap you in an immediate emotional response of defending the way you are. Try this instead:

- Say, "I don't know. I'd have to think about that."

This is a good aikido move because it blends with your mother's question, lets her know you heard it, but it doesn't take the bait and create more resistance by trying to answer it. Instead, it redirects it to neutral territory. You really would have to think long and hard to answer an emotionally loaded question like that.

This is such a powerful technique because it gives you the choice of dropping it, which is what you'd want to do with this question, or thinking about it and responding to your mother later. Either way, you're off the hook.

- Another good expression is: "I don't have an answer for you. I'll have to get back to you on that one."

There is great power in admitting that you don't know something because your mother (and other people) often lie in wait to challenge you on what you do know. It's another way to avoid taking the bait and give yourself the time to make a calmer response.

My sensei told me how important it was to set certain patterns of movement in my body, to develop a sense of flow in my techniques. She said when done properly, the techniques move naturally with the skeletal and muscular structure of the body as opposed to trying to force ourselves into more contrived movements.

Building a new relationship with your mother, one based on a more equal sharing of power, requires the same skill and patience. It may feel very unnatural, even contrived at first to give your mother these short responses, because you are so used to explaining everything to her. But if you practice these techniques and others I've mentioned, they'll become more natural to you. In time, they will become part of the new flow you are establishing with your mother.

Dropping the Apologies

Another way you may give your power away to your mother is by apologizing too much for things you didn't do. It's your way of making peace, of staying connected to her and avoiding the conflict.

It's important here to make a distinction between legitimate apologies and the apologies you use to smooth things over. Unless you have wronged your mother with your words or actions, there is no other reason to apologize to her. You do not need to apologize for expressing your emotions, for expressing your opinions, for standing up for yourself, for having a schedule conflict, or for saying no. When you get in the habit of apologizing for all these things, it's as if you are apologizing for your very existence, for if we follow your logic, everything you do must offend your mother.

The next time you are tempted to apologize, stop and ask yourself, "What am I apologizing for?" If you are trying to smooth things over or pacify your mother, realize you don't need to apologize—and make a different comment. Any attempt to apologize now, when you know you shouldn't, is a false-power move, a way of trying to manipulate your mother.

Expressing your true power requires that you know the difference between giving a communication that is true to yourself and giving one that manipulates others, and comes with the responsibility that you will not misuse your power to hurt others or mislead them.

TRY THIS

Perhaps you've just missed a big family dinner because of a previous commitment, and your mother is mad at you for not being there. The next time she sees you she says, "I guess I need to make an appointment with you to get on your schedule." Instead of apologizing for not being there, try this:

- Say, "I really wanted to be there. I'll look forward to the next dinner."

Once again, you've let mother know that you heard her, but you didn't take the bait and start apologizing for not being there. Why? Because you are a powerful woman and you know your own schedule better than your mother or anyone else does. Your reasons are your reasons, and you do not have to explain them to your mother.

By telling your mother you wanted to be there you are reassuring her that your relationship with her is important and that you value time with her. By telling her you look forward to the next dinner, you're letting her know you want to spend time with her in the future. This is all you need to say. Don't try to tell her to call you earlier next time, because you'll just be giving her something to argue about, and besides, the amount of notice she gives you might not make a difference.

This same technique can be applied to any number of situations and works best when you keep the focus on what you want (or wanted) and not on the erroneous belief that you did something wrong. It reaffirms your connection to your mother and allows you to move into other areas of conversation and relationship without a lot of explanation.

Being Able to Share Who You Truly Are

You know you are holding your power with your mother when you are just able to be yourself around her. Gone is the fear of getting her disapproval or losing her love. Gone is the need to mirror back the drama and power struggles. Gone is the desire to blame her, to rebel or procrastinate or make any of those other false-power moves. Gone is the need to second-guess your mother, the need to be so guarded in her presence.

Susan is cooking with her mother when she turns to see her covered with flour, making the worst-looking pie crust she has ever seen. She starts laughing and says, "Will you just look at yourself?" Her mother looks in the mirror and starts laughing, too. Then she tells Susan the pie crust is pretty bad and starts to make another one.

Susan hugs her mother and returns to cooking. Gone is the need to power it out with her mother. Gone is the need to take the job back and make the perfect pie crust. Amidst the flour and mess, she's found the greatest treasure of all, the ability to be herself around her mother and simply enjoy her mother's company.

One of the most telling lines in the movie *The Joy Luck Club* is when one of the mothers tells the daughter, "I see you." The daughter doesn't think her mother has ever seen her, has ever understood who she was, but her mother has seen her all along. It is a priceless reminder that the intimacy we've always craved with our mothers is right in front of us.

It's about time we let our mothers see us, that we become vulnerable once again and let them in. I say this to you not as the perfect daughter, but as one who hid from her mother most of her life. When I did let her see me, and I saw her, that's when things changed in our relationship. That's when I realized that I came from a long line of powerful women, and I was powerful, too.

You will experience that same power when you let your mother see you. And you will be free in that power when you can sit right next to your mother, to this woman you love and hate at the same time, and be comfortable with whatever comes up.

And Mama Makes Three:

Mama Drama and Your Marriage

I knew our marriage was in trouble from the beginning

when my mother showed up at our wedding

wearing a black armband.

Staying in the Picture

"I'll never forget my wedding," Georgia told me. "The photographer was setting up to take a picture of the wedding party, and my mother was so afraid she was going to be left out, she bolted clear across the dance floor, practically knocking people over, just to be in the picture. Even at my wedding she had to grab center stage."

Georgia's mother might have been more dramatic than most, but all mothers whose daughters are marrying face the same dilemma—now that their daughters are leaving them for good, how do they stay in the picture, the relationship?

You have to understand that your mother is torn at best. On the one hand, she knows this is the natural course of things, that all along you were supposed to grow up and get married. She may have even been preparing you like some prize for the most worthy suitor and probably had much to say about your husband-to-be. But your actual wedding was the turning point when your mother finally realized that she'd lost control of you once and for all, and that your husband, a stranger no less, is going to be having more influence over your life decisions from now on, when she had the primary part in doing so.

All along, your mother has wanted things to remain the same, and now she is forced to accept a change in your relationship, to face the fact that you love your husband just as much as you love her. She feels happy that you are starting a new life, sad about your leaving, and, most of all, displaced, wondering what her new role or position in your life will be.

You hope at this point that your mother has plans for a life of her own, that she'll write that book she's always wanted to write or find some other all-consuming life mission. It would make your departure easier on her. It would give her a chance to reassign priorities and put you more in the background of her life, if that's possible.

But if not, your mother may try to interfere in your marriage in a variety of ways, just for the sake of staying connected to you. When she does this, she thinks she's helping, contributing to the good life she wants for you. But you don't see it that way. You think she's out to sabotage your marriage, and your defenses go up. What's really happening is your mother hasn't learned to let go—she hasn't found her new place with you.

WAYS YOUR MOTHER MAY INTERFERE WITH YOUR MARRIAGE TO STAY CONNECTED TO YOU

- Making you feel guilty for leaving and marrying.
- Demanding loyalty to her and the family.
- Giving unsolicited advice.
- Prying confidences out of you.
- Invading your home with excessive phone calls/visits.

- Taking over when she does visit, instead of being a guest.
- Using money or gifts to control you.
- Becoming emotional or out of control when you and your husband disagree with her.
- Criticizing your husband, competing with him, playing him against you, so you'll retreat to her.

Buying into Your Mother's Criticism of Your Husband

There's an old Yiddish saying that goes, "It takes two people to make a marriage—the woman and her mother." Your mother would still like to arrange your marriage for you, if only you'd let her.

According to her, no man is good enough for you. That's why she often makes instant judgments about your husband. She wants to make sure he can provide you with the good life. You may have fallen in love with his potential, but your mother wants results. She doesn't want a medical student—she wants a doctor. She doesn't want a struggling entrepreneur—she wants someone who's already made his millions. The bottom line is she doesn't want your life mortgaged for a future that may never happen.

Your mother believes she has your best interests at heart, but she may be projecting her marital dissatisfaction onto you. That's why, throughout your journey of healing mama drama, it's important to keep asking, "Who is my mother?" If your mother doesn't trust men and is so unhappy in her own relationship, she won't be able to give you positive messages about your husband or marriage in general. You may never see her display the tenderness that's possible between husband and wife, because your mother doesn't know how to show you this.

One mother I know carried her distrust to an extreme by hiring a private detective to check up on her son-in-law. Why? Her own husband had cheated on her, and she was afraid her daughter's husband was doing the same. Her daughter never found this out until after her mother's death, but by then it was too late. Her mother had never trusted her husband, and this attitude was poison to the daughter's marriage, which eventually ended in divorce.

MAMA DRAMA MINUTE

Mother had a way of sizing up people in the first few minutes, and my husband failed her test. She didn't like the fact that he was a salesman without a real job. My brother had graduated top gun from a prestigious law school, and she had been grooming me to be First Lady or at least the wife of a lawyer or doctor. Quite frankly, my husband fell just a little short of her standards.

She never did forgive him for proposing to her daughter on a simple vacation or for taking her to buy her wedding dress in Tijuana of all places.

The only words she could seem to manage for her new son-in-law were: "Well, I know you're a good salesman. You sure sold Denise a bill of goods."

The first time she cooked for him, he ate only a moderate portion of food, another cardinal sin. When his brother ate more, she dismissed my husband by saying, "Your brother eats like a man should eat."

An avid believer in astrology, she was horrified that I married a Gemini like my father. This was all the evidence she needed in order to proclaim that she totally understood my new husband. Talk about the kiss of death! Since she didn't really respect my father, she transferred that same disrespect onto my husband, who resented being lumped in the Gemini pool and being treated poorly in the process.

I fooled myself into believing that my mother's comments didn't matter, that I loved my husband and could overcome her negative first impression. But the truth was that a lot of seeds of doubt were planted in those beginning messages: because he's a salesman, he won't be able to really give you the good life—because he doesn't eat like a real man should eat, he's a wimp—because he's a Gemini like your father, he'll hurt you like your father hurt me. None of these things were true about my husband, but the damage was already done. No wonder my husband joked if he'd met my mother first, he might have thought twice about proposing.

All of us couples starting out are presented with comments or events that could shape our relationships for life. It's how we handle them that makes the difference, and handle them we must, or our impossible mothers, along with our other in-laws, will define our relationships for us. The enemy isn't really them, but the conflict we create with them and allow to spill over into our relationships.

DRAMA TRAP: ALLOWING YOUR MOTHER'S CRITICISM OF YOUR HUSBAND TO AFFECT YOUR RELATIONSHIP

If you buy into your mother's criticism of your husband, you will poison your own marriage by undermining the love and trust between you and your husband. You will create a dynamic where your mother feels she can manipulate you further and where your husband feels he must fight your mother to save his marriage.

You have to understand that your mother's mission to go after your husband is her unhealthy way of staying involved in your life. It's as if she's trying to make up for her unhappy marriage or life by making sure your husband gives you a better life. When this happens, she is temporarily making your husband into her husband and is determined to fix him. She wants you to participate in this mission because it gives the two of you something to share.

If you are foolish enough to buy into her criticism and manipulations, you will set a whole series of problems into motion that will only trap you in a no-win situation in your marriage. By repeating your mother's criticism and making her sound like an authority on the subject of your husband, you are giving your husband the wrong message that you believe your mother over him. He can't help but feel betrayed, like the one woman who should be his ally has joined her mother against him. This makes him feel so angry, upset, and out of control, that the only way he knows how to respond is to declare war on your mother.

At this point your mother and your husband enter into a major power struggle, where each one intensifies efforts to get control over the marriage and you. Because men are by nature problem fixers, your husband may try a number of strategies such as criticizing your mother, separating you, or cutting you off entirely from the relationship.

Where does that leave you? You get lost in the battle and feel alienated from both your husband and your mother. You know you created this mess, but you don't know how to fix it. You realize you should be loyal to your husband, but you can't totally abandon your mother either. You can't entirely cut her out of your life without feeling like you've cut off part of yourself, and if you try, you end up resenting your husband for it and that resentment can destroy your marriage.

To break free from this nightmare, you must be willing to take responsibility for defining and maintaining your own relationship with your mother apart from your husband. You must accept your part as cocreator of this drama and realize that you have left yourself and your marriage wide open for attack with your actions. You must resist the temptation to tell all, what your mother said about him, what he said about your mother. You must keep your husband out of the conflicts and not try to hide behind him when things get tough with your mother.

TRY THIS

Make it a point never to repeat something negative that your mother said about your husband and his family. Why? Because each time you do, you chip away at your husband's self-esteem.

Rabbi Joseph Telushkin, in his book *Words That Hurt, Words That Heal* (see Resources Section), refers to such comments as "negative truths" (*"lashon ha-ra"* in Hebrew, meaning bad language or bad tongue), because they hurt people, lower self-esteem, and ruin reputations.

You may think there's nothing wrong with telling your husband something negative if it's true, but it will still hurt your husband. Rabbi Telushkin advises us to eliminate such types of speech from our relationships, along with spreading rumors, lies, or gossip.

Read his powerful book for a variety of strategies on how to choose your words more wisely.

The relationship your husband has with your mother will key off the relationship you have with her. If you handle your mother and leave him out of it, he will be able to enjoy your mother more, and you will have a much happier marriage. If you side with your mother against your husband, he will fight back for his own survival and make your mother, and possibly both of you, the enemy. The choice is yours. You must define your marriage before your mother's criticism defines it for you.

Forming a New Ring with Your Husband

IMAGINE THIS

Imagine that your marriage is like the rings that form when you drop a pebble in a pond. Before you married, you and your husband came from separate rings with your parents in the center. Now that you are married, you and your husband must form your own ring and put yourselves in the center. Your parents will now take their place in the outer rings of your life, along with any children you may have.

When you decide to marry, you must accept the fact that your relationship with your mother will change, that she will move from center ring to one of your outer rings and take a more supporting role in your life. Notice that you don't drop her from your life—she still has an honored place in one of your rings. But you do form your own ring with your husband and give your marriage top priority.

Some of us have no problem doing this. We've already formed our own rings by going away to college, by traveling, or by starting a new career. These good-byes helped us overcome any separation anxiety we may have had at leaving our mothers. I have one girlfriend who, at age thirteen, told her parents she didn't want an allowance anymore, that she was going out to get a job. When it came time for her to marry, it was no big deal with her mother, for the daughter had already been fiercely independent for years.

But some of us, because we were raised to stay with our mothers, may find it more difficult leaving them and creating our own lives. We don't have a clear enough sense of ourselves to fully imagine a life with our own rings, let alone live that life. Even when we're twenty-five hundred miles away we feel like we've never left, because we haven't separated from them emotionally. When this happens, we may be tempted to split loyalties between our mothers and our husbands, hoping that it will never come back to bite us, but it always does. It is this very flaw, this inability to separate that keeps us stuck in the drama we want to escape.

There are still others among us who have no intention of leaving our mother, because life with her is too good. Mike complained to me about his ex-wife Jill saying that she never would form that ring with him, because she was too attached to her mother's purse strings. Whenever Jill wanted something, all she had to do was ask her mother for it, and she'd get it. This started with clothes and gadgets, then extended to baby furniture, vacations, college funds for the kids, and even a house.

The problem wasn't her mother's generosity, but the way Jill handled it. She never separated from her mother enough to allow Mike the chance to do these things for her. Even when she and Mike would agree to wait and save to buy something, she'd go to her mother to have it sooner. Eventually, the marriage crumbled because Mike couldn't deal with Jill's inability to separate from her mother, which he called her *eternal maternal obligation*.

What was the payoff for Jill? As long as her mother was footing the bill, she never had to grow up and face her own life. She could remain the darling of her mother's family and hide out in the comfortable life her mother had provided her.

Forging an Alliance with Simple Rules and Procedures

Once you accept the fact that your relationship with your mother has to change priorities, you are free to forge an alliance with your husband and develop some simple rules and procedures that will help you maintain both a happy marriage and a good relationship with your mother. An alliance is an agreement that you make with your husband that says your relationship comes first, and you don't violate the covenants (rules) of that relationship for your mother or any other family member.

Marty and her husband did forge an alliance early in their marriage and have always been able to keep a healthy perspective on her mother. She and her husband are well aware of the games her mother tries to play, but they use code expressions like, "It's Mom being Mom again," to buffer her effect on them. They share the attitude that her mother is this storm that will blow over and it isn't worth getting upset at each other. They simply have never allowed it to interfere with their relationship.

The worst problems they have with her mother is during her visits when, instead of being a guest, she wants to set the entire schedule and take over their kitchen. Since they both understand this is her mother's pattern, they allow her to blow in and take over for a while until she finally mellows out with them.

Mike's marriage failed because he and Jill never forged an alliance that their marriage came first. Without this foundation, there was no trust and support for making the simple rules and procedures that could have saved their marriage.

When he and Jill were expecting their first child, they found a baby crib they wanted which was expensive, but affordable if they decided to save for it. They agreed to put some money aside every month and buy it closer to the baby's due date. One day he came home from work to find the crib bought, assembled, and placed in the exact spot his wife's mother thought was best in the nursery. He was so hurt all he could say was, "Didn't you think we could do this together?" Jill just ignored his feelings and made some excuse about her mother wanting her to have it right now.

What Mike and Jill should have done was made a simple rule like "No major purchases unless we both agree" and a procedure for implementing the rule: "If you or your mother want to make a large purchase for us, let's discuss it first." Notice that there's some flexibility here. He's not saying that he won't accept a gift from her parents—he's simply asking to be included in the decision. Why?—because he doesn't want gifts being used by his in-laws as a tool to manipulate him, because he wants to buy certain things for his wife himself. These are legitimate concerns for making such a rule.

Mike wanted Jill to honor him as her husband by bringing him into the decision and standing by the decision the two of them made together. But because Jill could never do this, and instead chose to go back to her old patterns with her mother, their marriage never survived.

TRY THIS

The next time you and your husband identify a conflict area with your mother, sit down and come up with your own simple rule and procedure for handling it.

For example, both your mothers want you to come home and visit them for Thanksgiving, but you and your husband have your hearts set on a scuba-diving vacation. You're tired of stressing out about your vacation because your mothers are both vying for your time.

Rather than get upset, you make a simple rule that you will make joint decisions about your vacations and not commit each other to family vacations unless you discuss it first.

That night you regroup over a bottle of tequila and decide that your marriage needs fun in the sun more than another visit with either of your mothers. You agree on your procedure, that you will each tell your own families what you've decided, instead of putting each other in the middle, and that you will make plans to celebrate the holidays with your respective families before or after your vacation.

A few tips about simple rules and procedures:

- Keep them simple—if you need a parliamentarian to interpret them, they aren't simple.
- Make sure you both agree to them.
- If there's a breakdown, don't overanalyze the situation. Just go back to the rule.
- Don't communicate the rule to your mother, just the decision.

If you focus on the rule and not the decision, you may find yourself explaining too much to your mother or, worse yet, asking her permission for something you've already decided to do. You do not need to tell her your rule about making joint decisions on vacations, especially when these vacations may take you away from her. This will only upset her and make her feel like you're pushing her aside even more. You simply need to tell her that you'll be in Barbados for Thanksgiving and make another time to visit her.

It's important here to make a distinction between using simple rules and misusing boundaries as most of us understand them. Simple rules are guidelines (your internal policy) that you make individually or as a couple to streamline communication and interactions with your mother. They work best when you do not communicate them to your mother, because she may feel a need to fight against your policy. Boundaries are limits you place on your mother's (and other people's) behavior to avoid experiencing pain or discomfort. You may feel compelled to communicate them to your mother in an effort to stop her from doing something that hurts you. For example, you may say, "Mother, if you don't stop talking about my husband, I'm going to hang up on you." It is a failed strategy, because you are asking her to enforce your rule, and she isn't going to do it. You may stop her all right, but not before she's already dumped on you to a certain point, and not before she got your emotions rolling. I don't recommend that you do this, because you will just give your mother something to argue or fight against.

Instead, make a simple rule that you don't gossip about your husband or his family, and if she starts criticizing your husband, change the subject or tell her you have to get off the phone to do an errand (your procedure). You can sidestep a lot of drama without rubbing your rule in her face. She may get mad at you because she can't discuss your husband with you, but that's her problem. You follow your rule without having to communicate it to her, and you protect your marriage in the process.

Anne and Rick: Late-Night Sessions of Conflict Resolution

The best way Anne and Rick learned to quiet the mama drama in their lives was to engage in late-night sessions of conflict resolution. Anne was raised in so much control and drama that she had few skills for resolving conflicts of her own. She was used to a constant undercurrent of tension, to her mother storming off and leaving problems on the table, and these dynamics carried over into her relationship with Rick.

So Rick insisted that if they had an argument about her mother or anything else, they would sit down and talk about it until something was resolved. At first Anne resented this exercise, because she was used to staying mad for days, to acting out in all the ways her mother had showed her. But Rick insisted they not go to bed angry at each other, so sometimes they would sit up most of the night before they could settle the problem. Eventually, the sessions became shorter as he and Anne became better problem solvers. And Anne saw the value of these sessions when much of the drama dropped away from their lives and she was able to have a better relationship with both her husband and her mother.

Their simple rule was "We don't stay mad and leave problems unresolved," and their procedure was "We stay up as long as it takes to resolve the problem." Even though they both didn't agree to this rule and procedure up front, they both agreed later, as they saw the positive results it had on their marriage.

Letting Your Mother Play the Martyr

Once you've truly separated from your mother, formed a ring with your own husband, forged an alliance that your marriage is the top priority, and developed simple rules and procedures for handling her, you can now turn your attention to your mother herself, to inviting her back into your life on different terms.

You have to realize that she has played the martyr with you, made sacrifices for you her whole life, and one of the best ways you can redefine your relationship with her is to let her play that role again. If your mother doesn't have her own life mission, you must create one for her and frame it in such a way that she will feel needed, like she's making a sacrifice for you all over again. Once you do this, she will feel a part of your life again and the energy she could spend nagging you, making your life miserable, is put to better use.

One busy career woman used this technique beautifully to have her mother plan her wedding. She started with the phrase, "I hate to ask you this, but . . ." and she immediately had her mother hooked. (Your mother likes nothing more than to be needed.) She went on about how she knew this was a terrible inconvenience (remember, your mother has to feel like she's suffering for you) with her mother's golf and bridge schedule, but there was no one else she could ask (she's really got her mother going now, because she's the only one who can save her daughter), so she was wondering if her mother could help her organize a few wedding details.

That's all this woman had to say, and her mother was off and running. Her mother enlisted the support of her sisters and the whole committee met on a regular basis to plan a spectacular wedding for her daughter. Her mother was happy because she was needed again, and this kept her busy for months. The daughter was happy because her mother was busy and didn't have time to interfere in her life or upcoming marriage, and the wedding turned out beautifully.

If you're thinking this is manipulative, consider the alternative, letting your mother interrupt you, bug you several times a day because she's bored and wants a place in your life. It's better to point your mother in a direction and send her off on a holy crusade.

Why do I know this will work? Because I heard this idea field-tested with several mothers on a San Diego radio station last Mother's Day. The station was running a "Mother May I," contest where they were asking daughters to make impossible demands on their mothers and then see how long their mothers took to say yes to the request. The disc jockeys were actually timing the mothers to see which ones said yes the fastest, and in every case, the mothers said yes. This was all done in fun, with great prizes for mothers and daughters alike, and yet the message was strong and clear—ask anything of your mother and she'll do it. Why?—because she's your mother, and she loves making sacrifices for you.

TRY THIS
You may not have a wedding to plan, but you probably have some other project or mission that your mother would enjoy. Call her up or see her in person, and say, "I hate to ask you this, but there's no one else who can help me. Would you be willing to _____ (whatever)?" Let your mother do something for you, and you just might find your whole relationship with her improving.

Once you start playing with this you may find your mother is so engaged with your new missions for her, she doesn't have time to bug you, or she may get tired of the work and decide to take that world cruise after all. Either way, you're off the hook, and your mother is one happy camper. What would you rather be doing, fighting with your mother or enjoying the time you do have together, because your mother is feeling good about having a place in your life?

Educating Your Husband About This Mother Stuff

There are a few great mysteries of the universe like the G-spot, the difference in tampons, and this mother stuff that might warrant further explanation to your husband. If you're lucky, your husband had a good relationship with his mother and he'll be more accepting of your need to stay connected to your mother. If you're not so lucky, he might be having trouble with his own intense mother, wondering how he can handle her so she doesn't interfere in your marriage.

He might have come to the marriage with a message from his father like, "Take a good look at your wife's mother. Your wife will look just like her one day." This message has almost become a joke among fathers and sons, but it is so insulting to the woman because it sets up conflict with her mother from the very beginning of the marriage. It makes her an unwilling pawn in a drama that says whenever she does anything that resembles her mother, she will upset her husband. It assumes that she is doomed to a certain body type and appearance, which she isn't. And it makes her feel guilty about being her mother's daughter in other ways, which she is and can't deny.

If your husband was given a message like this, gently take him aside and explain to him that many of the qualities he initially loved in you came from your mother. Share with him how important it is for you to maintain a connection with your mother for your own sense of security and well-being. And reassure him that being your mother's daughter is a blessing, not a curse as his father might have told him.

If your husband gets mad at you, and says things like, "You look just like your mother," or "You sound just like your mother," don't fight back or shrink away in disgust, but say, "You better believe it—isn't it great?" His comments are only more false attacks, because you can't deny that you are your mother's daughter, so why fight against it? Somehow, in those tender, quiet moments with your husband, you must tell him how much it hurts you when he says these things and ask him to see the good qualities you share with your mother.

If your husband wants to cut you off from your mother, remind him that you will never be happy being alienated from her, that you are better off limiting your relationship with her, rather than eliminating it altogether.

Too many times we involve our husbands in the drama without giving them the understanding of our relationships with our mothers and we leave them ill equipped for handling the emotional fallout. We expect them to do for us what we may not have been able to do ourselves, quiet the conflict with our mothers. Educating them, not lecturing them, in these ways is actually an act of love that could save our marriages.

When I grieve for the casualties of mama drama on my two failed marriages, I have so much more empathy for both myself and my husbands because on one level we didn't know any better. We were simply living a relationship as we'd seen our parents do it, and they weren't always the best role models. We didn't have the perspective to stop and confess how much the drama was hurting us, because we were too busy reacting to everyone else.

We often don't get that perspective until it's too late, until our marriages are over and we have no other choice but to lick our wounds, and ask, "What really happened there?"

When my first husband David came back into my life, it had been over seventeen years since we divorced. His wife had graciously given him her blessing for the visit. I wasn't prepared for the emotions that consumed me, for the feeling that time had somehow stopped and we had come full circle in our lives to heal our pain once and for all.

Because I was writing this book, our conversation naturally drifted to our mothers, to the ways these powerful women had shaped our futures. I told him how hurt I was when his mother took me aside, and said, "If you want to go to graduate school, just tell my son to hold off giving you the ring for a while." He never knew his mother had said this to me, how much it hurt me to give up my own dreams. I thought I had told him this, but I hadn't.

It is the things like this that we leave unspoken that cause us the most pain. By not telling him, I sent my resentment underground and, halfway through medical school, we divorced, for a number of reasons, one of the most important being I never handled this issue with him. I wished I'd found a way to tell him how important my dreams were to me and enlisted his support in making a plan where we could both go for our dreams together. We might still be married today.

For the sake of your marriage, don't hide your feelings from your husband. Let him know how this key mother-daughter relationship plays into your life and reassure him that you are committed to making the best of it, so it doesn't interfere with your happiness.

A Better Ending to the Story

David and I had long since forgiven our mothers and ourselves for the failure of our marriage, but we still needed to hear the apologies from each other. I told David that I was so sorry I never truly left my family for him, that I didn't know how to be a tender loving wife to him. And he told me that he, too, had failed to be a proper husband to me, to love and cherish me the way I deserved. He said if he had humbled himself to God and shown me the true face of love, I would have been better able to give the same to him.

There have only been a handful of times in my life when I felt the piercing presence of unconditional love, and this was one of them. I finally understood how special the love between a husband and wife could be and knew that his visit was a gift sent by God to give me hope for a relationship in the future.

When I told my father what happened between us, he said he was happy for both of us, that it put a better ending on the story. That was actually what it was. David wanted to affirm to me that our marriage, mama drama and all, wasn't that bad, and that in spite of our individual failings, we had each contributed to the other's growth and well-being.

If there is one gift I can give you, it is this—at any given moment in your life you, too, have the opportunity to write a better ending with both your husband and your mother, to quiet the drama that's invaded your life and robbed you of your own happiness. It is my deepest wish that your story will not end in divorce, but will continue in the kind of sacred love David was showing me, the love of a man and his wife who form their own ring and still have enough love to include their mothers in the circle.

We all need men who will love us for being our mothers' daughters, who are secure enough to let us embrace the best of our mothers and forgive the worst, men who will lead us toward that sacred relationship we both deserve.

And the men in our lives need no less from us—that we be whole women instead of wounded daughters, women who can be more present with them because we have settled our mama drama, women who can share our lives with such passion that we spark the divine in both of us.

To these better endings, I dedicate this chapter.

Conscious Parenting: Minimizing

Mama Drama in the

Next Generation

When I had a baby, I told my mother I bought the classic

Dr. Spock parenting book, *Baby and Child Care*. "I hope

you bought it in paperback," she said. "Why?" I asked.

"Because it's just the right size to give her a good swat

on the behind."

The More We Think We Know, the Less We Know

A parenting instructor once began his lecture with the following story: "Before I had kids, I taught the ten rules for effective parenting. When I had my first child, I taught the five suggestions for effective parenting. When I had my second child, I taught the three possibilities for effective parenting. By the time I had my third child, I stopped teaching effective parenting."

Can't we all empathize with this parenting instructor? The more we think we know about parenting, the less we actually know. Before I became a parent, it was easy for me to put my mother in the hot seat and criticize her for being too harsh. It was easy for me to say that I would never make the same mistakes with my kids. But I changed my tune when I had children of my own. I never realized how much time and energy it took to raise them. I never realized how difficult it was to keep my childhood out of my parenting. I never realized how humbling it could be to fall short of ideal parenting on a regular basis.

Actually it was the quest of ideal parenting that tripped me up the most. My mother had told me that being a mother was the toughest job I'd ever have, that before I knew it, it would be over and I'd have only one chance to do it right. So there I was, out there trying to do it right all the time, terrified to make a wrong move, because, after all, I was writing a book on mothers and daughters, and if I couldn't do it, who could? I was so determined, I wasn't just trying to do it right for my daughters, I was trying to make things right with my childhood. Eventually the whole thing became exhausting, and I felt I knew less than when I started.

Luckily my subconscious kicked in and gave me a dream.

There was a great drama being rehearsed in the middle of the ocean, high atop a platform. I can't remember all the characters in the play, but there were definitely lots of feminine archetypes performing their roles. I was asked to audition for the part of mother (surprise, surprise), but first I was told by a voice that I had to climb several steel links, triangular in shape, to get to the top of the platform.

I began climbing frantically and the more I moved, the more I realized how uncomfortable I was, that I was afraid I wouldn't make it to the top and would lose the role. I was starting to work myself into a frenzy when I realized I didn't want to struggle, that it was OK for me to stop and go back, that I could just be myself. This actually came to me not as a thought, but as a feeling of knowingness that was so profound, it immediately took my fear and anxiety away.

As soon as I climbed back down, there was acceptance from the voice that I had made the right choice for myself and had still won the role.

I'm sure a Jungian psychologist could put a nice spin on this one, but my analysis is quite simple: I had trapped myself into believing there was only one way to be a mother, and I had set this as such a lofty goal, it was literally something I had to be willing to climb up to. The fact that I hadn't yet won the role of mother meant that I hadn't yet accepted myself as the mother I was, when other parts of me (the other feminine archetypes) were already getting free expression. The voice was my intuition that knew all along I didn't have to strive so hard to be the mother I wanted to be. It affirmed my choice as the right move for me, the one that gave me the coveted role of mother. Finally I was free to experience being a mother in whole new ways.

The journey of becoming a conscious parent is very much like my dream. It is a process of bringing to our awareness those unconscious beliefs that may have trapped us into striving for an ideal or into passing on the same sense of drama to our children. It is the stripping down of what we think we know to see what is right in front of us. It's throwing out the rules that don't work for us and making up others as we go along. It's surrendering to those times we feel the most vulnerable with our children and finding joy in that surrender.

Effective parenting isn't doing it right, it isn't striving for an ideal we'll never reach—it's being conscious of the choices we're making, it's being in the moment with our children who are our greatest teachers. This is not something we can achieve, but something we are here to experience.

> Too many people define success to include parenthood or personal happiness. That is a mistake. These things are not a competition. You can't "succeed" at motherhood, for example. There is no first prize.
>
> —Bonnie St. John Deane,
> author of *Succeeding Sane* (Simon & Schuster)

The Trap of Unconscious Parenting

Meryl Streep was being interviewed in *USA Today* about her character Lee in *Marvin's Room*, when she said, "I really understand Lee, trying to control her son and making just about every wrong move there is. So filled with outward determination and hope, and inside being so self-loathing and visiting that on her kid. The last thing you want is the worst part of you to be continued in your children. And that's exactly what she does. She turns him into someone who hates himself."

Like Streep's character, the last thing we want is our drama to spill over into our children's lives, but it does, if we remain unconscious to the fears and emotions that are motivating our parenting. Sometimes it is self-loathing—we're so tough on ourselves, we don't know how to be any different with our own children. Sometimes it's guilt—we feel we did something wrong, and the only way we know how to make up for it is to be harder on our children. Sometimes it's fear—we're so afraid of certain things that the very things we fear come upon us. Sometimes it's pride—we're so determined to be better mothers than our mothers were to us that we are shocked to hear their exact words come out of our mouths.

DRAMA TRAP: GOING ON AUTO-PILOT
WITH YOUR CHILDREN

You remain an unconscious parent when you automatically react in emotional, nonproductive ways, usually triggered by your own childhood experiences, instead of making calmer, grounded choices in the moment. When this happens, you may resort to the same old tired tactics your mother used with you, such as screaming, spanking, and treating your children disrespectfully.

Paula's Story: Parenting out of Guilt

Paula was seventeen when she became pregnant with her oldest daughter and married the baby's father. Soon afterward, she had a second daughter. "I started out wanting to be the best parent, to prove to others that I could do something well," she confided, "but I was parenting out of guilt for my teenage pregnancy. I wanted to do the right things to have perfect kids and make them into super Christians," she added. She was trying "to right her wrong," as she put it, by looking good through her children.

But the marriage was doomed from the start. She and her husband came from different ethnic backgrounds that were difficult to reconcile, and he became abusive. One night, he told her the dinner was no good and threw a plate of food at her in front of her daughters. That's when she left.

There were many tough parenting moments. "My kids didn't know how much I cared about them," she confided. "I was out of control, angry, yelling and screaming at them, mad that they weren't cooperating. I didn't think they appreciated me, and I didn't know how to tell them how I felt."

While she was separated from her first husband, she met another man, eventually married him, and had a little boy. This time both her marriage and her parenting were much better experiences for her—she was older and had learned from her earlier mistakes; she had survived the trauma of divorce and reestablished a strong family unit, and both she and her husband were committed to learning more about parenting. They took several STEP parenting courses (see Resources Section), began practicing the techniques, and eventually became parenting instructors themselves. They still teach courses today, helping hundreds of parents improve their parenting skills.

When I asked her what she had learned about parenting the second time around, she told me it was the importance of expressing her love to her son. "Every day I tell my son how precious he is, that I'm honored to be his mother. He knows he's loved," she said. She admitted she wasn't able to do this as easily with her daughters when they were younger, because she was more unconscious in her parenting, overcome with emotion and fear, and upset in her marriage.

She told me that, like her, many parents make the mistake of parenting out of their fears. She credits her faith with helping her overcome her fear and likes to quote the Bible verse, "Perfect love casts out fear" (1 John 4:18). Her advice to parents: let your child solidly feel your love. The more you can do this, the better relationship you'll have with your children.

TRY THIS

Dr. Ralph Kellogg teaches color-coded communication, based on the work of Dr. William Purkey, in which compliments are identified as blue cards and criticism is identified as orange cards (see Resources Section). Criticism is so powerful, it takes twelve blue cards (compliments) to make up for every orange card (criticism) we give our children. If our children hear too much criticism instead of praise, they will not believe the praise when they hear it, because they just won't trust it.

Become a "blue card" mother by trying these things instead:

- Spend some time each day just holding your young children, alone or with their blankets to reassure them of your love and affirm them in a nonverbal way. As Paula reminded us, our children need to *feel* our love for them.
- Focus on what your children do well, instead of what they do wrong. Find something praiseworthy in each of your children and do not compare them with each other.
- Praise your children for different qualities and accomplishments and change the order of your praises.

Children have a tendency to take the first thing they hear as the most important, and that's why it's important to change the order of your praises. For example, if you tell your daughter that she's beautiful all the time, she may grow up putting too much importance on her looks over her other attributes. It's fine to tell her this, but also tell her she's powerful and smart and capable and loving, and change the order, so she can feel that these qualities are important, too.

- Give actual blue cards to your children by writing them words of praise on 4"-by-6" blue index cards.

Dr. Kellogg's business card is a blue card that folds in half and opens to blank lines where he can write compliments to the people he meets. He gave such cards to my daughter Meghan and me at a speech contest, and we still treasure them.

Some parenting courses teach parents to encourage rather than praise their children, based on the belief that too much praise can make our children more approval-seeking and accomplishment-driven. When in doubt, err on the side of praise. It is much better than giving your children too much criticism.

To shift from unconscious to conscious parenting, we, too, must understand our motivations. Are we simply imitating our mother's style of parenting? Are we parenting out of anger at our ex-spouse? Are we trying to compete with other mothers? Are we parenting out of sheer exhaustion?

We must also take a look at where our story line and our children's story lines cross and make sure we aren't parenting out of a reaction to unfinished business from our own childhoods. These motivations may be more hidden from us if there are certain painful memories we've been wanting to block out. We may experience them as feelings of general irritability or favoritism toward one child who makes us feel better or worse in terms of our childhood script.

For example, we may be driving for our daughter's field trip and get upset when the other girls don't just flock to our car. Part of this emotion comes from wanting to protect our daughter and part of it comes from remembering the pain of us being picked last for team sports. At this moment, it doesn't matter that we're the adult—we may feel the pain all over again. When this happens we have to become conscious of that memory, get a quick emotional handle on the situation, and not allow it to interfere with the time we're sharing with our child. If we don't do this, and remain unconscious in our childhood pain, we could overreact to our own child and make matters worse.

Paula had some tips on how to bring these fears and childhood scripts to the surface:

- Deal with yourself first.

Take an honest look at your own parenting style compared to your mother's. Ask yourself if you're imitating her martyrdom or her perfectionism with your children. Ask yourself if something from your childhood is bringing extra emotion to the dynamics.

- Question everything you do as a parent (your habits and practices), but don't beat yourself up about any negatives.
- Find replacing behaviors for the things you don't like, and practice them until they become new habits.

Remember, these fears, motivations, and scripts only become a problem for us when they go underground, because then they stay hidden from us and we can't do anything about them except act out with our children. But once we bust them, bring them to the surface, we can decide to change them or let them go.

Sheila's Story: Your Greatest Fears Come upon You

"I raised my girls believing that everything should be fair and that's a big trap, because it's not like that," Sheila explains. "If one got something, the other one got it, there was no difference—but there is difference in the world. The underlying issue was I didn't want them not to like me or be mad at me, and this really tinted the nature of our relationship."

When Sheila's youngest daughter was in high school, she fell in with the wrong crowd, a group of wealthy kids with lots of toys but little involvement with their parents, and she started partying a lot and skipping school. Eventually, she became suicidal. "I had to realize that her talking about suicide wasn't just talk. I put her in a hospital for observation for a week, which wasn't a popular thing to do. We went through a lot of turmoil, resentment, and hate, and I don't think any parent wants her child to hate her. We avoid that feeling at all costs. Suddenly my greatest fear was upon me, and I realized she might hate me, but I wasn't willing to take the risk of her being serious about this threat.

"Our whole relationship changed around that week we were in the hospital. She saw that no matter what, I wasn't going to let her go down. I hated that expression 'tough love' and felt that parents who did that were mean, but I was not about to outlive my daughter, to let her go off the deep end. I didn't want to lose her."

Sheila stayed by her daughter's side and even took on the school officials who weren't going to let her daughter graduate. When her daughter walked across that stage to receive her diploma, Sheila was so thankful for her life and their relationship. She continues to be the closest to this daughter, of all her daughters, because of the crisis they survived together.

Sheila's motivation for parenting was wanting her kids to like her, and her greatest fear, that they might hate her, was exactly what she had to face to become the parent she always wanted to be. It was her love and commitment to her daughter, that perfect love Paula spoke of, that cast out the fear and brought both Sheila and her daughter to a deeper, more authentic relationship.

We can learn something from this story, namely that our greatest fears may be the very beliefs standing in the way of us becoming the parents we've always wanted to be. When we have the courage to face them head-on, and invite these broken parts of ourselves back into our lives, we, too, can become conscious parents like Sheila.

Setting the Practice of Becoming Conscious Parents

The study of aikido involves the practice of protocol, ceremony, and etiquette both on and off the mat. For example, when students enter the mat, they bow to the altar, which has several Japanese artifacts on it, along with a picture of O'Sensei, the founder. Bowing to the altar has no particular religious significance—it is merely a demonstration of respect for O'Sensei and the martial art itself.

One day my sensei took me aside and gently reprimanded me for being late to practice and for sometimes leaving early. She told me how important it was to set the practice, to start by kneeling quietly before the altar, bowing to the sensei, and to end by bowing to the sensei and my partners. She explained that these rituals were like the markers that set the practice, the time in between, when we would be asked to demonstrate techniques and respect for the partners we were training with. I started to give some excuses, but she stopped me. She explained that we all have stresses and distractions, that part of the practice is learning how to leave those aside for the moment and empty ourselves to the training.

To truly live conscious parenting with our children, we must do the same thing—empty ourselves of anything that gets in the way of our parenting (our unconscious beliefs and behaviors), set a new practice of love and respect, and establish our own markers or rituals for reinforcing the practice.

There is no greater motivation for setting this practice than remembering that our children become what they practice. If they practice drama, they'll learn to live drama their whole lives and pass it on to their children. If they practice respect and kindness, they will extend those qualities to their children instead. When we raise our children, we're raising our grandchildren who come after them and, to some extent, all the future children in our families by the practices we set.

Specific Practices to Enhance Your Relationship with Your Children

To become conscious parents, you need to be specific with your children. You can't just tell them you want them to be good—you need to give them details and feedback about their behavior. You need to make a plan for the family and tell them what the plan is instead of keeping it a mystery in your expectations and criticism. And you need to be consistent in your actions.

Your plan does not have to be complex—it is simply what you want as a family (some would call this a *mission statement*), *rules of conduct* (behaviors you will and won't tolerate), *consequences of misconduct,* and a *system of rewards and punishment.*

Once you have a basic plan in place, you can focus on specific practices that will help you implement the plan and design the relationship you want with your children. These core practices are:

- *Care and Attention:*
  Give your children your undivided attention and care in the moment.
- *Sharing:*
  Share your life with your children, not just your money.
- *Respect:*
  Interrupt old patterns of criticizing and replace them with more respectful communication.

- *Regrouping:*
  Take time to withdraw and regroup when you're feeling exhausted or emotional.
- *Encouraging:*
  Drop the perfectionism and give your children room to fail (and succeed) on their own.

Care and Attention

Sensei Darrell Bluhm, in his article "Aikido and the Cultivation of Care" (*Sansho,* Aikido Journal of the USAF Western Region, Summer 1997), wrote about the value of practicing aikido to hone our skills of care and attention. He explained that in the martial nature of aikido there is a heightened awareness of life-or-death encounters which "wakes up our senses and sharpens our attention." At the same time, there is an environment of care, a "kindness that underlies this martial fierceness that is rooted in a commitment to bringing forth what is possible in the moment without concern for comfort, but with a strong commitment for safety." He also explained that care and attention did not mean being too nice to our partners, that we were still engaged in a martial art, and being too nice could actually put our partner in harm's way.

When it comes to disciplining your children, you must be willing to apply this same concept of care and attention. You need to care enough for them that you are committed to correcting them in the moment without concern for their comfort (safety yes, comfort no). You need to remain committed to bringing forth what is possible with your children, namely their more noble character and behavior. If you're too nice to them, if you want them to like you, you won't have the clarity—and yes, the fierceness to deal with the challenges that arise.

You must also be willing to wake up your senses and give your children your undivided attention, not attention that is split between them and some other person or activity. This means you give them full eye contact on their level, not looking down at them or towering over them, with periodic head nods to signal you are truly listening to them. It also means you clear the distractions away and stay with their conversation until they feel heard and understood. A few minutes of this kind of focused attention is worth more than several minutes of interrupted attention.

You can exercise your fierceness by demonstrating a willingness to correct your children in the moment, to match your intensity to the situation. Why is this necessary? Because too many of us take a passive-aggressive stance with our children—either we are lax and let them get away with murder or we are screaming at them or spanking them to bring them back into line. Your fierceness is actually your most caring move, because it quickly brings your children back to the appropriate behavior before their misbehavior puts them (and you) in harm's way.

To correct them in the moment, you need to bring them back to your rule, procedure, and consequence.

TRY THIS

If your daughter is in the habit of interrupting you while you're on the phone or in the middle of a conversation, try this instead:

- Make a rule that she can only interrupt you in a nonverbal way during a conversation.
- Give her a nonverbal cue (the procedure) to interrupt you, such as putting her hand on your forearm and you putting your hand over hers to acknowledge that you know she wants to talk to you.
- Tell her that the consequence (the punishment) for breaking the rule is an hour of restriction on play or television after school or give her some other consequence.
- If your daughter follows the rule, find a way to make a comfortable break in your conversation to give your daughter your full attention for a moment, then resume your conversation. Reward her by giving her some special time alone with you.
- If she interrupts you without following the rule, ignore her behavior, finish your call, and then give her the punishment (one-

hour restriction of play or television). Don't argue with her, explain yourself, or defend your position.
- If she protests further, bring her back to the rule and use the "From now on" expression: "From now on I want you to use our hand signal if you need to interrupt me."

Your effectiveness with this technique will depend on your ability to stay fierce in the moment, to give it your full care and attention. If you vacillate and cave in, you will be sending the message to your children that you can be manipulated and overruled. If you hold firm, you will actually see your children's behavior improve.

Sharing

My favorite advertisement is the AT&T commercial in which the kids are bugging their mother to take them to the beach and she says she can't, that she has a meeting with a client. Her daughter stands right in front of her, and asks, "When do I get to be a client?" Her mother knows she's caught—she can't resist that line, starts laughing, and gives her kids five minutes to pack up for the beach. The commercial ends with the mother conducting her business meeting from the beach on her cellular phone, surrounded by a pack of giggling kids.

When do your children get to be your clients? When do they get to have your time and fit into your schedule? If you're like most parents, the answer is: not very often. You may keep your children and yourself too busy to spend any real time with them, dragging them from one activity or errand to another, putting them in the latest class, taking them to the latest movie. You may buy them the latest toys—the videos, the computer games, the rollerblades, thinking this will substitute for your time, and then wonder why they're so mad at you because you're too busy to play with them. You may think you have to do all these things to be good parents, but that is just another trap of unconscious parenting. The truth is, your children simply want to spend time with you.

Your busyness could be just another excuse to avoid your children. Maybe you stopped playing years ago and dismissed this kid stuff as foolishness and being with your children is too painful a reminder of what you left behind. If that is the case, you, even more than your children, need the play time.

Whatever your excuse or distraction, your children need you. They can't become as close to you as they want unless you spend time with them. It is your words, not the baby-sitter's, they want to hear reading the bedtime story or singing the lullaby. It is your hands they want stroking their hair. It is your presence they want as they drift off to sleep. There are no substitutes for this.

You have a choice. You can stay busy, continue to put your children as a second or lesser priority, or you can set aside time to be with them and build that closeness in your relationship. You may not always feel in the mood to play with them or even like the things they want to do, but still you must try, because it is the connection you are making with them, not the activity itself, that's important.

My most satisfying moments as a parent are when I surrender to what my daughters want to do and see where that takes us. Those are the times we create candlelit baths that last for hours or build sand castles at the beach or lie on a blanket and look up at the stars. You can have those same moments with your children when you drop the busyness and just relax with them.

TRY THIS

- Set aside special blocks of time to be with your children.

Put them in your calendar in a special color and keep them as you would keep any other appointment. For that time, your children are your most important clients, and no one or nothing else is more important.

- Ask your kids what they want to do during their time with you.

If you need special materials to do a project, buy them before your time together, so you do not have to run out and do an errand. Remember, you are cutting down on the busyness.

If you are a single mother and share custody, ask your kids what they want to do the next time they see you, so they can be anticipating the fun they'll have when they come back. This will help them make transitions between households.

• Block out all other distractions and enjoy.

No parent ever said on their deathbed they wished they'd spent more time at the office, but many have said they wished they'd spent more time with their children. Their guilt comes from thinking they somehow wronged their children by not being there for them, but the truth is they are the ones who missed out, even more than their children. Take the time now to be with your children so you don't have regrets later.

Respect

You may have the best intentions of treating your children with kindness and respect, but still fall into the trap of overcriticizing them. Understand that criticism is a bad habit, perhaps leftover residue from your upbringing, and you can correct this once you realize that you're dealing with a pattern.

It begins with a comment or action your child makes which triggers a feeling in you and makes you feel out of control. You think it's your children's behavior that offends you, but it's really the way you feel that is so upsetting. At this point, your self-critic comes in and starts getting mad at you that you can't handle the emotion better, so instead of turning your anger on yourself, you direct it to your children. Before you know it, you're hurling words at your children so fast, they can't keep up.

This cycle can be greatly reduced or avoided altogether when you allow your children to interrupt the pattern. One way you can do this is to give them a simple, neutral expression like "JJ's in the jam jar" which is a code expression that means "Mother, you're scaring me, please stop." Explain to your children that they can use this anytime they're feeling overwhelmed by your criticism. Why is that important? Because they, better than you, know if they're feeling overwhelmed. You may not think you're upsetting them at all, but they may be feeling your anger. They must have a way to protect themselves. Don't be surprised if their threshholds for fear are different.

If your children use the code expression, you must stop and withdraw from the conflict, take time to regroup, and talk to them later when you are calmer. You cannot give your children an expression like this unless you intend to honor it and do your part.

The beauty of this code expression is it allows your children to interrupt the nonproductive behavior (your screaming, your nonstop criticism or raging) without having to explain themselves or engage in an argument with you. It teaches them that no one, especially their parents, has the right to rage at them, for if they grow up taking this disrespect from their parents, they will come to expect it from their friends, spouses, coworkers, and bosses. And they will also learn how to lash out at others. That's how toxic nonstop raging can be.

When you do come back from regrouping, you need to refocus your attention to the offending behavior, not the rap (the criticism, the raging). Simply bring them back to the agreement you previously made with them (your rule). Do not start criticizing or raging again.

For example, if your daughter is fighting you on doing her homework, because she wants to go out and play with her friends, instead of getting into a lot of dialogue, go back to your agreement with her. Say, "We agreed that you would do your homework first before you play. When you are done with your homework, you may play with your friends."

TRY THIS: THE CLICKING TECHNIQUE

Another pattern interrupt that is effective in preventing the downward spiral of criticism is the clicking technique. This is used when either you or your children go into an automatic behavior that takes you down the same path of conflict, a behavior that you've already corrected with your kids or one they've already interrupted with you. It is especially helpful when you are yelling at each other, raging out of control, or arguing without resolution.

BUY SOME PLASTIC CLICKERS ON A STRING (OFTEN SOLD AT NOVELTY STORES OR STREET FAIRS).

The clickers are symbols for both you and your children that you each have the right to speak, that your feelings are equally important, and it gives you a neutral object and sound to interrupt the pattern. (If you can't find the clickers, you can snap your fingers to make a sound, but the clickers are more neutral, because they aren't attached to a person like your fingers are.)

ESTABLISH SOME GROUND RULES FOR USING THE CLICKERS, NAMELY THAT

- You click twice at the offending behavior,
- You stop talking for a moment (30–60 seconds to regroup),
- You immediately go back to the agreement (rule).

(NOTE—This technique is to be used after you've already agreed to the rules in your family meeting. It is not meant to be used every time you discipline your children, but rather for those specific times mentioned above.)

Example: You Clicking Your Children

You ask your oldest daughter to pick her clothes up off the floor and she says, "How come I have to do it? Why don't you make my sister pick up her clothes? You're always getting mad at me."

You can tell you're going down a familiar path of conflict, so you click twice and your daughter stops talking. You wait a moment, then calmly say, "We're talking about you picking your clothes up, and we've agreed as a family that we will each pick up our own clothes and put them in the laundry hamper." (Notice that you don't take the bait and start discussing her sister.)

Example: Your Children Clicking You

Your sales presentation bombed and it appears that you have lost the account. Your boss wants to see you first thing in the morning, and you are not in the mood to handle anything more. Before you even say hello to your children, you begin snapping at them, carrying your bad mood into the family. Your daughter clicks you twice. You get quiet for a moment, and she says, "Mother, you promised you wouldn't yell at us after work. You agreed to take a break if you needed it." (Now if you can get her to draw you a hot bath, you really have it made!)

WHY THIS WORKS.

This works because nobody wears the blame. When you click, it says to both of you, "We're doing it again. Let's get back to the real issue," and this message is conveyed to you without a lot of words. There's no need to get into a lengthy discussion, because you've already discussed the rule at another time when you were both more calm. You cannot make rules in the heat of an argument. This technique simply brings you back to the rule you've already established.

If you do get caught in discussing something too much, you can agree, "From now on (Remember the power of this expression to point you toward the future), let's use the clicker in this situation to get us back to the point."

This technique stops the blaming, the endless stream of criticism that can be so damaging, and gives both you and your children a chance to regroup. Don't think this technique is just child's play. It has been used effectively between arguing couples and between secretaries and their bosses.

You must remember that you are not just disciplining your children, but you are instructing them in respectful behavior. If you treat them with more respect and let them interrupt your disrespectful behavior, you will find over time that you will be able to break yourself of any negative patterns and you will receive more respect from your children. If you are a parent who likes to control your children, this may seem scary at first, but over time you will establish a new foundation of love and respect, and this will be well worth your efforts.

Once you stop the criticism and other disrespectful behavior, you need to find other means of communicating with your children that are more positive and encouraging. Some of the best I've found are:

GIVE THEM TWO CHOICES.

Instead of trying to overpower them, give them two choices and let them decide what to do. Tell them you trust them to make the right choice for themselves.

ASK THEM A QUESTION.

If they ask your advice about something, turn the question back on them, and ask, "What do you think you should do?" If they say, "I don't know," ask, "What would you do if you did know?" Empower them to find a solution.

PRAISE THE EFFORT, NOT JUST THE RESULT.

Encourage your children when they take steps to become more self-sufficient. Instead of looking for the perfectly made bed, say something like, "I noticed that you're starting to make your bed. I appreciate your efforts to organize your room in the morning."

Regrouping

When parenting breakdowns occur, they are a sign that you are moving too fast and are out of touch with what's happening in the moment. Instead of screaming or spanking your children, you need to stop, give yourself a time-out, and regroup. This is the only way you can see options for yourself.

Whenever possible, remove yourself from the situation and announce to your children that you will be in your room for fifteen to twenty minutes and will come back out when you feel more calm. Your children may not know how to take this at first. They may try to follow you into the room and bang on your door because they are afraid you have abandoned them. If that is the case, give them an egg timer set for the time you need and return to your room. Tell them they can wait outside your door, but they are not allowed to make noise to interfere with your quieting time. If you find you need more time, go back to your children and tell them what you're doing and take the time. As long as you reassure them you're fine and will come back out, they should settle down.

This technique works if you are in the middle of a conflict and need to withdraw immediately to calm down. But it's even better if you become proactive about your regrouping practice and create islands of time for yourself every day.

TRY THIS

- Set aside some time every day, even if it's just for fifteen to twenty minutes, to regroup away from your children. Use the time to read, relax, recharge yourself for the next round of parenting duties.
- Jan Connors, owner of Art & Soul, has developed a set of eight "Memos from Mom" doorknob hangers (see Resources Section) which you can use to signal your children that you're having one of your breaks.

Each hanger has a picture of a mother doing something, like taking a bath, so even young children can look at the picture and understand what their mothers are doing. And for the little readers in your family, the memos give further instructions. For example, the reading memo says, "Mom loves you very much, but ... MOM IS READING ... You may enter only if you have your own book!"

When you give yourself a time-out to regroup, you are setting a powerful example for your children that they can do the same, that they don't have to wait to be punished to go to their rooms. You are showing them the importance of self-quieting and self-nurturing, important practices they need to become happy, calm adults.

Encouraging
Encouragement seeds your children's dreams and makes it safe for

them to venture out into new territory. It gives them unconditional love and support and frees them to discover who they truly are. You know you are a conscious parent when you can encourage your children in what's good for them, instead of what's good for yourself. Brad Rutledge is such a conscious parent. After seeing his daughter falter in a piano recital, he reassured her that he was proud of her for keeping her cool and getting back on track. In his essay, "Room to Fail Brings Success," his words echo every parent's vulnerability at allowing the less-than-perfect move in their child.

I'm a dad, and naturally I would have loved to see my daughter perform flawlessly. But when she didn't, I was as proud as a parent could be to see the character well up in her and give her the wherewithal to finish what she had started. I realized as I watched her just how strong and determined she is, and how important this will be to her when she is an adult.

It seems to me that we give our children precious room to fail. With all the subtlety of a cymbal crash we send them the same message again and again: succeed, succeed, succeed. Get good grades. Be first string. Get into this college or that one. Get a high-paying job. Get promoted. Succeed.

The irony is this. The focus on success is really a focus on an end. But the ability to succeed (including happiness in the measure of success) is ultimately dependent on process. If one can enjoy the process of an activity, fill it with passion and joy and draw from it the energy that sustains one's soul, one is likely to accomplish remarkable feats with much less angst. . . .

Since the night of the recital my daughter has not mentioned her flubbed performance. Caught up in the frenzy of sixth-grade life, she has put it behind her and moved on to other adventures. And though she doesn't know it, each time she succeeds at what she does, or gloriously fails in the effort, I do what I did that night: I give thanks all over again for this wonderful person God has seen fit to make my daughter.

Brad had no trouble arranging his priorities: daughter over performance, daughter over success in the traditional sense. He didn't need her to succeed to make him look good. Because he was conscious and knew who he was, he was able to extend that freedom to his daughter and truly encourage her.

For you to give your children true encouragement, you must do the same: allow your children to make less-than-perfect moves, praise the effort, not just the result, and have a clear enough sense of yourself, that you are free to put your interests aside and focus on what's best for your children.

TRY THIS

Your daughter's teacher tells you that your daughter is becoming too dependent on you to do her homework and she actually suggests you back off and allow her to make more mistakes. You worry that your daughter will fall behind, but the teacher explains that she must be allowed to learn from her consequences. To allow the less-than-perfect move, try these things with your daughter:

- Encourage her to do her homework away from you, so you won't be tempted to hover over her every move.
- Acknowledge her newfound independence from you with a comment like, "I notice that you're working very well by yourself."
- If she comes to you for help, refocus her on doing it herself by saying, "I'm sure you'll be able to figure it out."
- Allow her to be responsible for her own homework and suffer the consequences of her not doing it or doing it incorrectly.

All the Right Moves

Even when we become conscious parents, we're not capable of making all the right moves. It just isn't possible. But we can make moves with love and awareness, and that's about as "right" as it gets.

Instead of chasing an ideal we'll never reach, we need to approach our parenting as an ongoing, loving practice and if anything, detach from both our fears about being less than perfect and our desires for specific outcomes with our children. Neither extreme will serve us. If we give in to our fears, we'll remain unconscious in our parenting. And if we follow our desires, we'll be equally distracted by things that may never come to pass.

Each day we have with our children, we need to control these fears and desires that interfere with the job of parenting and remain committed to handling whatever comes up in the moment. When we do that, we remain conscious and are free to move with our children wherever they take us. I'm not sure where my children are taking me, but I know I am committed to the journey, to staying in the love, and minimizing the drama. Every day they teach me more and more about myself.

EIGHT

Facing Your Mother's Death:

The Moment of Truth in

Your Relationship

My mother says she wants to be cremated. That's her

way of getting me to do housework from the grave,

giving me one more thing to dust.

Donna Marie's Story: Shifting into Neutral with Her Dying Mother

Six months before Donna Marie's mother died, she confessed to her Al-Anon group, "I know I'm going to miss her when she's gone, but if she lives much longer, she's going to drive me crazy"—a very candid statement from a daughter who was feeling ambivalent at best about the death of her impossible mother. Donna Marie's mother was an alcoholic dying of severe diverticulitis, bleeding in the intestines.

An only child, Donna Marie had a long history of taking care of her mother, and now that her mother was finally dying, she wasn't sure how much more she could take. It started in her teens when her father died, and her mother began drinking heavily. For years she tolerated her mother's verbal abusiveness and moods, stuffing her own anger and resentment. She covered for her mother, never discussed the drinking with anyone, even cleaned up after her when she was sick. She did such a good job of hiding her mother's drinking, it would be years before she could admit the problem to herself and find her own help in therapy and support groups.

Even after Donna Marie moved away, she continued to make trips home to rescue her mother from the latest drinking crisis. She'd do her best to help her mother and take care of herself in the process, but these trips still left her emotionally and physically drained. Because her mother required so much help and intervention, Donna Marie decided not to have children of her own. She felt her mother was her child, that this was all she could handle.

When it became clear, on one of these trips, that her mother was dying and this was not just another rescue mission, Donna Marie made a decision to put her mother's affairs in order and relocate her to a nursing home, where she could receive loving care around the clock. She knew from their intense history together that she would never be able to care for her mother in her own home and remain sane in the process.

Once her mother was in the nursing home, she became easier to deal with because she stopped drinking, and her personality changed. Instead of being loud and abusive, she became more soft and gentle. This was a pleasant surprise for Donna Marie and very healing, for she had not seen her mother's sweeter nature in years.

The last visit with her mother was especially rough because she didn't know what to expect. "I had to shift into neutral—If my mother was ready to die, I had to go with that, and if she wanted to stay, I just needed to stay with her," she told me. Doing this gave her incredible peace, as she realized there was nothing for her to do but surrender and be with her mother. Before she left, she gently kissed her mother and said, "I'm fine, Mother. Don't worry about me. Just take care of yourself." Her mother died the day after she left.

To this day, Donna Marie feels totally at peace with the loss of her mother. She has no unfinished business, no sense of guilt about the relationship, but instead feels complete with the ending the way it happened. It wasn't perfect—she wasn't there clutching her mother's hand at her bedside, but there was really nothing else she would have done or said to make it more complete for her.

When it comes time for you to face your mother's death, you want to experience that same peace, be just as complete in your good-byes, just as complete in your relationship. You do not want to be left behind with a lot of unfinished business in your relationship that can't be resolved in person with your mother.

Facing Your Mother's Death Is a Series of Surrenders

Facing your mother's death is a moment of truth in your relationship when you come face-to-face with both your own mortality and the fact that time is running out to make peace with your mother. It's a time when you can no longer play the games, lie to yourself, pretend it doesn't matter, because death has a way of cutting through such delusions. It's the time you have to face losing two mothers, the one you have and the ideal mother you've always wanted.

All of a sudden you can't hide out in a bad relationship. You have to stop blaming your mother, stop using her as an excuse for everything wrong in your life and face your own life. You have to stop obsessing about her and deal with the issues death brings up. If you're lucky, you have time to say good-bye, time to finish the unfinished business. If you're not so lucky, she dies before you see her and you are left wondering what you could have done to make your relationship better.

Facing your mother's death is a series of surrenders, minideaths, which serve as stepping stones to the ultimate surrender of all, letting her go. When you allow it, this series of surrenders will lead you to a deeper awareness and acceptance of who you are, as you redefine yourself in the death of a woman who has shaped so much of your destiny.

Embracing the process, going where it takes you, will transform you and help you grieve her more meaningfully. Fighting it will attack you at the very core of who you are, and keep you stuck trying to make sense of it all.

These surrenders are:

- Shifting into Neutral
- Pacing Yourself
- Allowing Others Their Own Experience
- Holding Vigil
- Saying Good-bye
- Facing Your Aloneness

Shifting into Neutral

As Donna Marie showed us, the best posture you can take with your dying mother is to shift into neutral. This means you surrender any agenda you have around your mother's death, as well as any preconceived ideas about how you should be feeling and behaving. This means you stay in the moment with her and see where the moment takes you.

Your agenda is your program around your mother's death. It's such things as your trying to control the visits of the relatives or your telling other people what to say and do. It's your being attached to things happening a certain way. It comes from your wanting to protect your mother, even prevent her death, by taking control of everything.

MAMA DRAMA MINUTE

Your mother may have her own agenda and ask you to carry it out. When my mother was dying, she asked me to tell certain relatives not to visit her because she was too tired, so I started trying to control the visits and only upset my aunt and uncles. Finally, the hospital staff told me to ignore my mother's request, to let people visit when they wanted to, and they would control the flow if it was too tiring for her. It never occurred to me that I could disagree with my mother when she was dying. I was trying too hard to be her good daughter again and do whatever she wanted.

Whether you realize it or not, your preconceived ideas about how you should be feeling and behaving around your mother's death make up a death script of sorts. You may even have an actual image of yourself at your mother's bedside and certain words in mind that you want to use to say good-bye to her.

The problem with this is you may get upset when you can't live up to this image, when you have to confront the conflicting emotions you are feeling. One moment you may be mad at your mother, the next moment sad, the next afraid of her leaving, the next wondering why her death is taking so long. One moment you may feel like disappearing—the next, you won't be able to leave her bedside. When you shift into neutral and don't attach to things happening a certain way, you are better able to ride this emotional roller coaster.

In his article "Zen and the Way of the Warrior: The Battle of Interior Mastery" (*Sansho,* Aikido Journal of the USAF Western Region, Spring, 1996), Buddhist Vice Abbot Genjo Marinello described staying in the moment as *mushin,* the mind of no mind, "a mind that is not stuck on anything but prepared to meet everything (including our last breath)." This is the way you must face your mother's death, not stuck on any agenda or feeling, but prepared to meet everything, even your mother's last breath.

Pacing Yourself

A good midwife knows when to eat, when to rest, how to conserve her strength for the time she is needed the most, the actual birth of the child. You need to do the same—eat, rest, exercise, so that you can replenish yourself and return to your mother's bedside ready to be in the moment. Nothing can prepare you for the mental and physical exhaustion you are about to endure, and if you don't take care of yourself, you may collapse at the time you want to be there the most, your mother's actual death.

TRY THIS

Your mother may experience a long illness before she dies. You must learn to midwife yourself in these ways:

- Start with having some honest conversations with your husband, relatives, friends, boss, and coworkers about what you're experiencing and what kind of support you need.
- Ask your family and friends for help spelling you at your mother's bedside, covering your kids, making you meals, giving you breaks to exercise, get massage or other services performed that will replenish you.
- Ask one friend to help with travel arrangements, to stay on top of the best fares and car-rental prices for your out-of-state travel.
- Ask your boss for flex time in your schedule or a sabbatical from work to be with mother.
- Check your company's bereavement policy, and ask your boss if he's willing to extend bereavement leave with vacation time.
- Ask your coworkers for help with projects and offer to return the favor when they are in need.

When you face your mother's death, even the simplest tasks are hard to do. That's why it's more important than ever to midwife yourself, to get as many things handled as you possibly can. It will free you up to just be with your mother and experience the emotions without worrying about how the rest of your life will be organized.

Handling the work situation may be more difficult, as most companies are not prepared to offer family leave for a parent's illness or death—at the most they offer a bereavement leave of three days for the funeral. One woman I interviewed told me her mother and sister died within a month of each other and she was fired by her boss for having too many deaths in a month. Hopefully, you will have a more understanding boss and a good relationship where you can explore your options.

Allowing Others Their Own Experience
One of your most challenging surrenders may be allowing your relatives and spouse to have their own experience of your mother's death. They may say and do things that are hard for you to understand, and

yet you must let them deal with your mother's death in the only way they know how.

You need to understand that they may not have much capacity for dealing with her death and therefore may not be much help to you. I was upset that my husband never visited my dying mother, that he seemed to get angry with me after her death. The truth was our marriage was in such a sad state, he didn't have any more emotional capacity to deal with a dying mother or a grieving wife. And if I am honest with myself, I have to admit that I didn't have much capacity for dealing with his father's death a few years earlier. As much as we wanted to support each other, we weren't able to do it. The same may be true for you and your spouse.

You may also find that your relatives have very definite opinions about your actions. They may question your decision to medicate your mother so heavily. They may disagree with your decision to cremate your mother, instead of burying her. They may want their voices to be heard in your decisions. You may find yourself getting territorial here, insisting your mother is *your* family, not theirs, and that you alone have the right to make the decisions. That may be true, but still you need to be sensitive to these relatives and realize they have their own special relationships with your mother.

Sandy's mother had suffered a cerebral hemorrhage and was immediately put on life support. When extensive testing revealed there was no more brain activity, Sandy made the decision to take her mother off life support. One of her aunts flipped out, threw herself on her mother's bed, and began screaming that Sandy was a murderer. Sandy was an only child, and it was her decision to make, but she decided to include her relatives in the decision and ask them what they would do. After discussing it, they all agreed with Sandy, even the aunt who was so emotional.

TRY THIS

One of the things you may want to do to prepare for your mother's death is set up a durable power of attorney for health care, which gives you and your brothers and sisters the right to make final health decisions, such as life support, for your mother. Have a meeting with your mother before she's ill to discuss this power of attorney and other matters of her estate.

Some of the things your relatives may want to do around your mother's death may shock you. My mother's family was Bulgarian, and her relatives in the old country were accustomed to taking pictures of the corpses at the funeral. None of my relatives wanted to do that, but one uncle did want to take a picture of my mother in her hospital room, and this upset my father, who thought it was morbid and left the room. This upset my uncle, who couldn't understand why my father was so upset. I was actually OK with it, because I understood my uncle's need to remember her this way.

You may find yourself in a similar situation where the death practices of a certain culture conflict with the beliefs of other family members. Try not to take sides and judge either party. Remember that everyone is handling the death the best way they know how.

My cousin actually gave me the best advice—she told me that none of us can be completely responsible for what we do and say around a dying loved one, that we must forgive ourselves our temporary insanity. The more compassionate you can be to your relatives, the easier it will be for all of you to say your good-byes.

Holding Vigil

There may come a point in your mother's illness when you actually need to hold vigil for her and sit by her bedside throughout the night. This waiting can be very draining for you, because your mother may come close to dying several times and pull back out of it. With each close call, you may find yourself tensing, holding your breath, leaning closer so you don't miss her last moment. Hopefully, you have been midwifing yourself along the way and have some energy and stamina to deal with it.

In holding vigil, the surrender becomes the waiting itself and detaching from your fear of your mother taking her last breath. If you have developed your own quieting practice, you will have an easier time releasing to the silence. Your prayer or meditation will quiet you to the point where you will no longer fight against the waiting, but accept it and your mother's last breath as extensions of the peace you're already feeling. In this way you can remain deeply attuned to your mother and even if you never say another word to her, she will feel your loving presence.

You may choose, instead, to hold a more active vigil for your mother by doing certain things to connect with both her body and spirit.

TRY THIS

When your mother is dying, the very last sense to go is her hearing, so you may wish to try some of these things to quiet her mind and comfort her:

- Read her a passage of scripture or other meditative prose.
- Sing her a hymn or a favorite childhood lullaby.
- Play some soothing music.
- Whisper words of comfort or praise to her.

Touch is another sense that lingers on. You may wish to give your mother a loving touch in these ways:

- Gently stroke her forehead and brow.
- Softly kiss her cheek.
- Massage her feet, shoulders, and temples with essential oils.

Instead of letting the waiting wear you down and upset you, use it as a precious time to make one final loving connection with your mother. She may not be able to speak to you or see you, but if you do these things, she will still feel you with her.

Saying Good-bye

One of the hospice supervisors told me about an exercise they use to train new workers. They deal each worker a hand of cards which represents the elements of a dying person's world: her family, her house, her possessions, her health, her memories, etc. They then ask the workers to give up all their cards one at a time, explaining that this is the task of a dying person, to give up everything.

Once you understand that your mother has to give up everything, even you, you can appreciate why she doesn't want to let go. It doesn't matter that she had to let go of you at other times in your life—when you went away to college, got married, maybe even became a mother yourself. This is the big one. Now she has to let go of you for good, when every fiber in her being is telling her to hang on and protect you.

That's why Donna Marie's final words to her mother were so precious, "I'm fine, Mother. Don't worry about me. Just take care of yourself." She knew her mother didn't want to leave her, wouldn't leave her until she gave her permission to leave. So instead of putting her needs first, she comforted her mother by reassuring her she'd be fine. It was a beautiful act of selfless love.

Saying good-bye to your mother is your last chance to connect with her. How you choose to do it will affect the way you remember her and the way your mother's essence stays with you. This is the time to finish your unfinished business. It doesn't mean that you need to conduct a therapy session bedside, but you do need to take time to complete the relationship.

It is a time of speaking compassionate truths, telling your mother those things you've left unspoken, asking her the questions you've always wanted to ask, speaking your words of praise and love. It is not a time to bare your soul and express negative truths, those things that may be true about her but that would hurt her. It's not the time to fix the relationship or make her pay. It could be a time to make a confession or an apology if you can genuinely put your heart into it. When in doubt, use peace as your guide. If it will bring your mother more peace, do it. If it will make her more upset, let it go. You will not find the peace if you have to hurt your mother first.

MAMA DRAMA MINUTE

I remember asking my mother before she died what her greatest accomplishment was and she pointed to me, and said, "You and your brother." I

started crying, and said, "Really? I thought we'd disappointed you." She shook
her head no. I was so glad I asked that question and got the reassurance and
love I needed. I might have lived the rest of my life thinking I had disappointed
my mother. Instead, I had to face my own perfectionism and realize that I was
the one being too tough on myself.

What question have you left unasked? What words have you left unspoken? Find the courage to speak them now, so you can feel more
complete in your relationship.

TRY THIS

When you say the last good-bye to your mother, give her permission to leave
and reassure her that you'll be fine. Also speak the legacy of her life. Say something like, "Mother, I want you to know what it's meant to me to have a mother
like you. I've appreciated your sense of humor, your commitment to me, the
way you taught me to take a stand for what I feel is right, and I want to pass
on these qualities to my children. I will always love you and remember you."

The most compassionate good-bye you can give is one affirming your
love for your mother and honoring the legacy she has given you. It allows you to take the best of your mother's life with you, allows you to
grieve her without the baggage of unresolved conflict, and sets the
foundation for the new relationship you will have with her in your
memory.

Facing Your Aloneness

When you face your mother's death, you are venturing into unchartered
territory and can feel scared, alone, even abandoned by her death. Suddenly you will understand your connection with her better than you've
ever understood it before. As long as she was alive, she was your safety
net—she gave you the illusion of security that you weren't alone. Now
that she is gone, the illusion is gone, and you must confront your aloneness, your mortality, your life. It doesn't matter if you had a loving re-

lationship with her or if you hadn't talked to her for years. You will still feel incredibly alone because you no longer have access to her.

In some ways, nothing can ever prepare you for her death. It is something you have to experience alone. It won't matter how many people are there to share it with you, you will have to make sense of it yourself. Karen, another woman I interviewed, described this process as "unraveling yourself and weaving yourself again."

This unraveling can be a state of confusion, where the pot is stirred and everything in your life is up for grabs: your career, your marriage, your religious faith, your future goals. You may decide to stay home with your kids because your mother told you all good mothers stay home with their children. You may realize how short life is and decide to have another baby, or leave your marriage. You may start a whole new career because you're tired of putting your life on hold.

Your aloneness will put you face-to-face with the void, and it's up to you how you want to fill it. You can use it as a time of empowerment and make some conscious decisions to change your life for the better. If you do this, you may actually find yourself making vows or promises around your mother's death which will propel your life forward at warp speed.

Rosie O'Donnell was one woman who used her mother's death as a powerful motivator to reach her goals. In an article in the Ladies' Home Journal, *she explained, "My whole life revolved around my mother's death. It changed who I was as a person. I remember thinking when I was ten years old, if I was going to die in my thirties, what would I want to have achieved? It made me strive for my goals with a fervent passion.*

"After my mother died, if you wanted to express something painful in my family, you could only do it couched in comedy," she added. Rosie took this coping strategy, along with the sense of humor she inherited from her mother, and developed her own amazing career in comedy.

If you are not careful, you could use the void to make some negative vows around your mother's death. You could expect more of your father than he's capable of giving. You could take your anger out on your other loved ones. You could play it safe by making choices your mother would want for you, only to find that those choices weren't what you really wanted to do after all. This is a much more reactive way to fill the void that could leave you spinning in confusion for months or years.

TRY THIS

Use your time alone with your mother's death, your unraveling, to weave a new life for yourself and make a tribute to your mother:

- Resolve to step out of character and make one new decision about your life that you wouldn't have made before your mother died.
- Volunteer your time in hospice or another program that helps other families.
- Make a public gift in your mother's name —a scholarship, a donation to a specific charity or the performing arts.
- Write a memorial booklet commemorating your mother's life and distribute it to guests at her funeral.

You have an incredible opportunity to use your mother's death as a rite of passage for yourself, to take the best threads of her life and weave them into your life. You can experience your aloneness, the fear and pain it brings with it, and come through her death a much stronger woman.

Making Peace with Your Mother When She's Already Dead

I was speaking at a spa in Palm Springs and Ruby came up to me, and said, "Mama Drama? What's that about?" I answered, "Settling your conflict with your mother once and for all." "Once and for all?" she asked. "To do that, I'd have to go to the cemetery. It's easier that way—she won't talk back to me. You know, she's the reason I carry all this extra weight on me." When I asked her how long her mother had been dead, she told me twenty years. Talk about unfinished business! She's still raging at her mother and blaming her for being overweight. Her mother will never be able to help her with this one.

Edith confided that her mother had been dead fifteen years, but she still couldn't accept the way her mother had lived her life. Edith's body was so rigid with tension, I could see the toll this unfinished business had taken on her life. As soon as I told her she didn't have to agree with what her mother did, and asked her to let go, she sighed and dropped her shoulders. She really didn't want to carry this emotional burden, but she didn't know what else to do.

Sharon had such a controlling mother, she decided to change the location of her wedding and not invite her mother. She refused to take her mother's calls and got married without her. The wedding went off fine, but her mother died six weeks later. She has spent an intense year in therapy trying to resolve her relationship, because she never had an opportunity to resolve her conflict with her mother.

The problem all these women are experiencing is not being able to confront their mothers about their unfinished business. It's still possible for them to make peace with their mothers, but it is more difficult, because their relationships ended in conflict, and they no longer have a way to receive their mothers' love and approval.

DRAMA TRAP: UNFINISHED BUSINESS

It is more difficult to make peace with your mother after her death when you've left unfinished business in the relationship, because you can no longer resolve it with her in person. You can only imagine a different outcome, not actually see the changes in your relationship.

When we have unfinished business with our mothers, it makes it more difficult to grieve their loss and get on with our lives, because we are still mad at them. We never could see them for who they were, and now, with unresolved conflict, we have even more trouble accepting them. We are so used to giving our power away to them, we don't know how to do anything else. As long as we can believe our mothers failed us, we have them to blame for ruining our lives. Letting go of that would mean we'd have to face our own lives and make some changes.

So instead we create fantasy relationships with our mothers in our memory where they can still punish us and make us feel bad. That way we can continue to be mad at them and don't have to face our own lives. As long as we are doing this, we will never find peace with our mothers, because they will always be there to let us down or punish us.

The best way to overcome this is to match fantasy with fantasy. If you created an angry, punishing mother in your memory, you can create a loving, forgiving one instead. You do this by taking simple actions to reestablish your relationship with your mother in the present.

TRY THIS

Instead of trying to fix the conflict or relationship with your dead mother, try these things to define a new relationship with her:

- Go to her gravesite with some flowers and talk about the good things that are happening in your life, as if your mother were there to listen to you and support you now.

Note: do not talk about the conflict at her gravesite, because you will relive the pain and emotions all over again.

- Write a letter to your dead mother telling her all the things you admire about her, thanking her for the gifts of her life. Mail it to a friend and ask your friend to keep it, so you can feel like you truly sent it to your mother.
- Keep your mother's memory alive by putting out a special picture of her, by cooking a meal she liked, by wearing a piece of her jewelry or clothing, or sharing something she liked to do with your children.

- Write loving messages to your mother on some helium balloons and release them into the sky.

Another technique used by some gestalt therapists and hypnotherapists is to put the daughter under hypnosis and actually take her back to have a final conversation with her mother. The therapist creates a scene where the daughter walks into a room and sees her mother sitting in a chair. He gently taps the daughter on her forehead and tells her to begin talking to her mother. When the daughter is finished talking, he taps her on the forehead again and tells her she's now the mother and can talk to her daughter. The daughter, speaking as her mother, tells herself whatever she needed to hear from her dead mother. When she is done, the therapist brings the daughter back to herself and has her leave the room. When the daughter wakes, she will feel as if she had a real conversation with her mother, like she's created a new ending to their relationship.

TRY THIS

Make a new positive association with your mother's memory in this way:

- Lock on to a happy memory, a time someone gave you flowers or another special gift, a time when you wore a dress you especially liked.
- Allow yourself to feel the joy that comes up with this memory.
- Now picture your mother.
- Go back and forth with these memories in your mind until you get the same feelings of happiness when you picture your mother.

What you are doing is transferring the joy of one experience to your mother. This can actually change the way you remember her and feel about her.

These things work because they help you create a different memory of your mother, and they put your focus on the present which is the only place you can heal your pain. You cannot go back and correct the past, but you can choose what you want to remember about your mother and free yourself in the process.

Karen's Story: Transformed by Her Mother's Death

Karen was very traumatized by her father's sudden death when she was eight years old. Instead of telling her the truth, her mother told her, "Daddy's gone away," and Karen would sit for hours looking out the apartment window waiting for her father to return. She was about thirteen before she realized he was never coming back. Karen felt angry and disconnected from her mother for years because of the way she handled this.

When Karen learned her mother was dying, she told her therapist that she didn't want to experience the same trauma she had with her father's death, that she wanted to make a total connection with her mother before she died. She knew it would be difficult for her mother to communicate with her, but she still wanted to be near her so they could experience that connection, even if it meant they would have to experience it telepathically without many words. She decided to take a month sabbatical from her work and visit her mother, who was staying with a married sister.

Karen knew this wasn't going to be easy, that she was going back to an emotionally charged environment. She wanted to avoid confrontations with her alcoholic brother-in-law, and she wanted to stay away from the anger of certain past experiences with her mother. Before she left, she had to build up her strength for the trip.

One of the ways her therapist helped her do this was to create an invisible shield around her through a hypnosis session where Karen was given an image (the most perfect red rose and the peace, love, and warmth around it) to use when she became overwhelmed in the environment. Karen needed to use this image more than once to calm herself. "It was a tremendous challenge not to get angry in that environment," Karen confided. "But that connection with my mother was the most important thing in my life, and nothing was going to get in the way, including me."

When Karen arrived, she spent as much time as she could in her mother's room, sleeping there, playing bingo, sharing meals with her. "It was the best time she and I had together," she said, "because there was a woman-to-woman connection that existed between us that had never existed before. I knew she was my mother and I was her daughter and that she loved me very much."

Karen returned from her sabbatical with her mother feeling more complete than she'd ever felt in their relationship and was totally at peace when her mother died three months later. The night before her mother's funeral, she stayed in her mother's room, slept in her bed, even wore her pajamas to feel that connection again. That night she fell into the deepest sleep and had a vision of her mother with a beautiful madonna-like smile, standing at the helm of a ship. Her mother told Karen she was fine and encouraged her to keep doing the work she was doing.

When Karen awoke, she felt happy and refreshed, even more at peace with her mother's death. She went to her mother's funeral full of energy, ready to celebrate her mother's life, and even served as pallbearer so she could participate in the ritual of saying good-bye.

Karen feels that participating so personally in her mother's death transformed her as a person. "When I left her funeral, it was almost as if anything I wanted to be, do, or have was there for the taking. I felt so powerful," she told me. To this day, she is a passionate advocate of making peace with your mother before she dies, of participating in the dying process with her, because she knows the freedom and power that comes from the experience.

Preparing for Your Mother's Death by Living Peace and Completeness Now

Whenever a woman tells me a story of conflict with her mother, the most compelling question I can ask her is, "What do you want from her before she dies?" It jolts her into realizing that there will be an ending someday and gets her thinking about what she wants right now.

Since you don't know when that someday is coming, your best posture is to live that peace and completeness right now in your relationship with your mother. Every time you see your mother, decide what you want to share with her, what memory you want to create that day. If you live like this, you will be living in *mushin*, prepared for anything. You will still feel sad when she dies, but you will know that you have just been with her in loving ways and that completeness will comfort you.

You can fool yourself into thinking there will be an endless string of tomorrows to settle these issues with her. You can resign yourself to living in a stale relationship with her, but this will never be satisfying to you. It will be like licking the crumbs at the banquet table when you could have had the entire feast. It will leave you with a whole list of "if onlys" taunting you to a more perfect ending. There are no perfect endings or perfect mothers. There are only the endings you're given and the chances to do with them what you will.

TRY THIS

Start with the end in mind. Understand that your relationship with your mother will end one day. Let the certainty of her death motivate you to settling conflict sooner rather than later. Ask yourself, "If my mother were to die tomorrow, what would I want from her? What would I want to say to her? . . . share with her?" Work backward from these questions and create the relationship that you want with her now.

Ellen told me how relieved she was because she was living in peace and completeness with her mother right now and didn't think this was possible. By disagreeing with her mother and handling the emotional fallout, she became less afraid of her mother's death, because the peace was already there. "I thought making peace was going to be a deathbed experience for me," she confided, "but I have the relationship I always wanted now, and I'm so happy about that."

You too can have peace instead of waiting for your mother's deathbed by creating the relationship you want now, by living in the completeness of a relationship that's satisfying to both of you.

PART THREE

THE PEACE

NINE

Creating a New Emotional Legacy:

Changing the Way

We Take the Drama

My mother didn't have relationships—she took hostages.

That's the Way We've Always Done It

Once there was a young woman who married into a loving family and she was helping the other women in the family prepare a holiday meal. She watched as her mother-in-law opened a beautiful canned ham, cut off the end of the ham, and threw both the ham and the can away. *How odd,* she thought and wondered if she dared ask her mother-in-law why she did this. After a while, her curiosity got the better of her, so she asked, "Mother, why do you cut the end off the ham before you bake it?" and her mother-in-law answered, "I don't know. This is just the way we've always done it." The young woman took another sip of her wine and decided not to push the matter further, but it never left her mind.

Six months, later, when it was her turn to prepare the ham, she couldn't stand it anymore and decided to ask Babcia, the respected grandmother and matriarch of the family, about the ham. "Babcia, can you tell me why we cut the end off the ham?" she asked. Babcia got a funny smile on her face, as only grandmothers do, and she answered, "Why of course I know, darling girl—that's a family tradition. My mother cut the end off the ham to make it fit into her special roasting pan. She always thought the ham tasted sweeter if it was cooked in her pan." Suddenly the daughter understood, so out of respect for the family tradition, she cut the ends off her hams and even bought a special pan to roast them.

When it comes to mother-daughter relationships, our legacy is much like the legacy of the hams. It is a passing on of behaviors, beliefs, in some cases, family protocol, that we do without questioning from generation to generation. It often starts with one woman in our family, like Babcia's mother, with a word, a gesture, an action that has special meaning to that person. This woman is so committed to what she's doing that her passion spreads to the other women in the family who adopt the behavior as their own. Soon this behavior becomes part of the family tradition, and new women coming into the family learn to identify with the family by engaging in the behavior. Only when they cut the end off the ham (or whatever), like the mothers and grandmothers before them, will they be considered "good family," one of them.

Once we understand how powerful legacy is we need to ask ourselves, what is the legacy of relationship we've inherited from our mothers? Will the ham truly taste sweeter? Will we truly be satisfied with the relationship that was passed on to us? Or do we, like Babcia's mother before her, need to start a new legacy of our own?

I was hoping when I interviewed women with good mother-daughter relationships that they would be able to tell me the secrets of their legacies, but the truth was, most of them didn't know. They had just been identifying with the other strong, loving women in their families and practicing loving relationships so long, they didn't know any different. In fact, they couldn't imagine or identify with the drama many of the rest of us lived through. This didn't mean they had perfect relationships—they had their fair share of conflict, but the strong legacy of love in their families overshadowed the drama. If there was any secret, it was that they continued the practice of good relationships with their mothers, as their mothers had done before them, and their practice became habit, second nature to them, part of the legacy they were able to pass on to their daughters.

This led me to form some new beliefs about legacy, the first being that all mothers, even the most impossible, leave us some positive legacy. There are gifts in their lives that may have come wrapped in incredible pain, but gifts that are there for the taking nonetheless. Every woman I interviewed, without exception, could find these gifts in their mothers' lives, no matter how painful and conflictual their relationships had been. We can find them, too, if only we'll look.

My other belief was that we all have the power to create *a new emotional legacy* by changing the way we take the drama, replacing it with new, more loving relationships, and modeling those relationships for our children, instead of the old legacy of conflict. If we continue to practice the techniques given in this book and stay in a loving relationship with our mothers, we will create that legacy and drop it into the pipeline for our children and future generations to come.

We can create this new emotional legacy at any time. Some of us pick key moments—the upcoming birth of our children, or the pending death of our mothers, but we don't need to wait for these life-changing events. We can do it simply because it's our time, and we're tired of living in conflict with our mothers.

Why We Miss the Drama and Repeat the Legacy of Conflict

Once we start to create a new relationship with our mother and a new emotional legacy for our children, we may wonder if we'll miss the

drama and fall back into our old patterns of conflict. It's a very legitimate fear and one that may create some problems for us if we don't understand the pull drama has had over our lives.

Drama is an old dance, but one we are more familiar with, one where
we at least know our defined roles. It is an addiction that gives us the
juice, an actual high off the emotions and adrenaline pumping through
our bodies. It makes us feel more alive, more normal. It changes our
brain chemistry and hormonal levels so much, that when we remove it
from our lives, we may experience an actual withdrawal of sorts which
can leave us feeling bored, sad, even depressed.

Drama is the great deceiver—it fools us into believing this is the
way life should be, exciting, full of highs and lows. It convinces us that
we are somehow better than others because we can live on the edge
and ride these highs and lows. We get so good at creating drama in our
lives and attracting people who will play in the dramas with us, that we
think we like it—we think it's what we want.

And, like any other good junkie, we can't stand the withdrawal.
When we remove it from our lives, we have to feel the bad feelings, we
have to face the void it creates in our lives, we have to face ourselves.
So instead of living with our uncomfortableness, we rush to fill the
void with more conflict with our mothers. We go back to our old patterns with them. We try to fix our relationships, make them see things
our way, because at least we understand the drama—we don't understand the peace yet.

But this drama, no matter how satisfying it feels at the moment, is
never a solution to our relationships, and we exhaust ourselves, rob
ourselves of our very lives by staying in it. There will only be a draw to
go back to this drama when there is an absence of meaningful relationships with our mothers and other people in our lives. When we fill
the void drama leaves, with new, meaningful relationships, these relationships give us renewed energy and passion and reduce the cravings
for more drama. These relationships are like nicotine patches that tide
us over, help us handle the withdrawal, until we can fully embrace the
peace that comes from creating our new emotional legacy.

When we truly experience that peace, it will bring incredible joy, gratitude, and meaning to our lives. It will bring us the "aha" in our existence, the surprise we've been waiting for so long.

MAMA DRAMA MINUTE:

Just a few short weeks ago my "ahas" started dropping in big-time. "Aha! I'm no longer arguing with my daughters." "Aha! I'm happy." "Aha! My life is running smoothly." "Aha! I'm finally meeting men who appreciate the goddess inside me." It was as if the fog had suddenly lifted and I was living the life I always wanted and at the same time creating a new legacy of empowerment for my daughters. For months, years even, I had been creating the space to redefine myself, my life, my relationship with my daughters and finally, it was here. I sat back for a moment and felt that strange feeling of calm. So this is what it's like, I thought. "Aha!"

For a moment, I panicked. Can it really be this good? What if the other shoe falls, and I'm right back in the drama again? I had just met a woman who spouted off more dramas in a few short minutes than I could ever imagine, let alone handle. *That used to be me,* I thought. *I lived in that space of drama, and I'm never going back there.* "Aha!"

Then I allowed myself to exhale and take another breath and go back to the calm. I realized that once I knew where it was, I could go there anytime I wanted. "Aha!"

Christine's Story: Changing Mother's Indifference to Caring

It isn't often that I have the chance to interview the same person every month for brief periods of time, but that was the case with Christine. We have been developing a friendship as she cuts my daughters' hair. At first our talks were just casual, about our kids, and then one day she asked me what I did for a living. When I told her I was writing this book, she began to tell me pieces of her story.

This past year she had a baby boy and she wanted her mother to know her child in a way that she had never known her mother. When I asked her if her mother was indifferent to her, she said yes, that her whole life, it was as if her mother was going through the motions. "I think she became a mother because that's what she was supposed to do," Christine said. "She was a librarian, and I think she had a whole other secret life in books away from us kids."

In previous conversations she had told me how she wished she and her mother were closer, how she wanted warmth and love and intimacy between them, but that it just wasn't there.

She confided that during her pregnancy her mother was just plain disinterested, and yet she made a decision to stay in touch. "I called her every week and rattled on about the changes in my body, all the medical stuff that I knew made her uneasy, but I still shared it with her," she said. "I never gave up. My husband would ask me, 'Why are you doing this? You're just going to get hurt.' Many times, I'd get off the phone and just cry." She knew the relationship wasn't happening, but she still had hope.

She was disappointed that her mother didn't come out to see the baby when he was first born, but instead decided to bring the baby to her mother. The visit had been OK—she was still hoping for more. When Christine returned home, she continued to call her mother and tell her about the baby. She began preparing a videotape of her son's first few months that she planned to send to her mother.

The next time I saw Christine, she told me her mother had received the tape and loved it. Her mother was starting to take more interest in her grandson. She told Christine she planned to come out in the spring to see the baby. But when spring came, she delayed the trip again until the summer. Christine called her mother up and told her that the baby was just too cute and that they would come to visit her, so she wouldn't miss this stage of the baby's life.

This visit went even better, and her son did his first crawling at her mother's house. Her mother enjoyed the visit and became more excited about her grandson. When he and Christine returned home, she called to tell them she missed them. Slowly but surely her mother was becoming more intimate with both her daughter and her new grandson. The last time I talked to Christine, there were even better developments. Her mother had started a mutual fund for the baby. She and Christine had been talking about the baby's schooling, that Christine wanted to send him to a private Catholic school, and her mother was offering to help. Her mother was still planning to come visit during the summer.

Christine is the first one to admit that she doesn't have a perfect relationship with her mother, but it's the best it's ever been. Over weeks and months of calling and through periodic visits, she has been making the space for her mother to shift from indifference to caring. It hasn't been Christine changing her mother, but Christine creating the space, the safety, the trust, for her mother to change herself. Christine's contribution has been an intense desire for her mother to have a better relationship with her child than she did with her.

The ultimate benefit of Christine's investment of time, energy, and love is the new emotional legacy she has created for her child. But also, by putting her focus on what she wanted for her child, she created new possibilities for her own relationship with her mother, who is now beginning to express the caring Christine always wanted from her when she was a child. It is difficult to say which behavior is the by-product of the other, but the truth is, it's working, and that's all that counts.

By changing the quality of what she and her mother shared, Christine changed the relationship. And everyone is benefiting from this newfound peace and intimacy. Her mother feels closer to Christine and the baby. The baby gets to know his grandmother and have her as an active presence in his life. The husband can stop worrying about his wife's phone conversations with her mother. And Christine feels more loved and nurtured by her mother and the ways her mother is loving her child.

What if it were that easy for us? What if we could consciously decide to drop the struggle and shift our course and fire it up with our intense desire and pursue the relationships we want so relentlessly that we weren't willing to settle for anything less? We can decide to do all of these things and more when we are committed to creating a new emotional legacy.

Staying in Your Practice with Your Mother

One of the things I love the most about aikido is this concept of practice. We come to practice several times a week to the point where this practice becomes a way of life for us, part of our internal discipline. We practice to the extent that there is no difference between what we do on the mat and off the mat—it is all part of the same thing, the way we interact with everyone and everything. We practice until the techniques become part of us. We never learn it all. We never arrive. We practice until the day we die. There are other students and masters further along in their practice than us, but even they haven't mastered it all.

When we are creating our new emotional legacy we must keep this concept of practice in the forefront of our minds. Everything we say, feel, and do around our mothers is practice. We may think our comments and actions aren't noticed or appreciated, aren't really making a difference in our relationships, but they are. They are all part of the legacy we're creating. No act of love or kindness is wasted, even when the result we want doesn't appear right away. Our mothers may need time to let our practice marinate inside them before they feel safe being a different way with us. Then, when they're ready, they may surprise us, like Christine's mother did, and act very differently in the relationship.

A visiting sensei described our practice as a yeast that bubbles and activates inside us until it comes out in our essence, in all our dealings with ourselves and other people. This is exactly what happens when we stay in practice with our mothers. The relationship we want begins to activate inside us until one day we do have evidence of things working differently with our mothers.

One woman declined an interview with me because she said she was feeling less than inspirational about her relationship with her mother. She had lost the peace in their relationship when her mother moved closer to her and became ill. Instead of enjoying their time together, they found themselves in more conflict. I appreciated her honesty and reassured her that if she would stay committed to the relationship, she would find her way back to the peace.

Just like this woman, there will be times in your relationship with your mother when you'll feel less than inspirational about her, and when these times occur, you must remember that they are part of the practice. They are there to show you the contrast between peace and conflict. They are there to give both of you opportunities to heal. If you stay in your practice, you'll find the peace again.

Mary's Story: Creating a More Meaningful Relationship with Shared Growth

Mary was eight years old when she had a serious bike accident in which she fractured her left leg, face, and neck. Her mother stayed by her side, giving her emotional and physical support. Mary described their relationship as somewhat normal, that they had their typical mother-daughter stuff and weren't really that close. She rarely asserted herself with her mother or questioned things, but went along with whatever was happening.

Years later she went through a series of surgeries to restore her body from the accident. When she was twenty-one, she went in for surgery and had a near-death experience on the operating table. "I went down this tunnel of light and instead of my life passing before me, I felt a complete understanding of it, without judgment. I felt I did well and was ready to go on. Then the light pulsed into a golden color and told me I'd have to go back. I told it no, which was so strange for me, because I never told my mother or anyone no. The light pulsed again and told me I had to go back, that there were people I would touch with my story. All of a sudden I slammed back into my body like I was slamming into a wall, and I was in pain again," Mary explained.

"This experience gave me a knowingness that there was more to my existence than my body and mind, that this experience of life and struggle wasn't meaningless, that there was a purpose to my life. It gave me incredible faith in God. After that, all my relationships became more meaningful," she added.

When Mary described this experience, her mother went to the library and got books on near-death experiences, reincarnation, and a number of other spiritual subjects. Mary and her mother began studying these books, going to lectures and meditations, and doing their spiritual seeking together. "It was not until I had my near-death experience and had a stronger sense of myself that the relationship with my mother turned into a valuable relationship, because we were pursuing growth together," Mary explained. Mary's whole personality changed as she became the leader on these spiritual quests and continued to bring the significance of her experience into their relationship.

Mary has still had her moments with her mother, times when they haven't talked, times when they go back into their normal mother-daughter stuff, but this life-changing experience continues to be the basis for their new relationship. "It doesn't matter if we're making spaghetti sauce or pursuing our spiritual path, it can still get messy," she confessed, "if someone needs to be right, but when we keep on growing, it can be beautiful."

Mary's near-death experience was a wake-up call that the way she was living her life and relationship with her mother wasn't serving her, and she was able to change her relationship by building on a shared interest of spiritual growth. Although she doesn't have children of her own, she continues to share this new emotional legacy in all her personal relationships.

Building a Legacy with Today's Actions

From Mary's story you can see that it doesn't matter what the vehicle for change is, you can create a new relationship and legacy when you build on a foundation of shared dreams, interests, or growth. Christine's shared interest with her mother was her son, the grandchild. A whole new relationship with her mother was possible once they shared the excitement of this child.

Every exercise I've given in this book has been designed to bring you closer to yourself and your mother, to make it safe for the two of you to have an intimate relationship. True intimacy is the ability to share your dreams, interests, and growth together in an environment of trust and safety.

So much of the rhetoric of our times has been about telling our mothers what they can't do in our lives, by giving them our boundaries for respectable behavior. The trouble with boundaries is they are good fences—they may keep certain behaviors out, but they may also keep us from the relationship and intimacy we want.

When you have true intimacy with your mother, you invite her into your life, not because she is so deserving of it necessarily, not because she's on her best behavior, but because you know you can handle whatever comes up. You don't worry about what will happen when she crosses one of your boundaries, because you have confidence that you can be yourself with her, disagree with her, and still stay in the relationship. You accept her for who she is and you accept yourself as well. You have nothing to prove to her, nothing to try to fix in her.

So how do you create this intimacy and build the legacy that comes with it?—by putting your focus on today's actions as an investment in that legacy. You do it by being fiercely committed to living the relationship you want with your mother today, realizing that you are creating tomorrow's memories. Erica Jong referred to this as "inventing memory" in her book, *Inventing Memory: A Novel of Mothers and Daughters.*

You do it in these ways:

- Finding a Shared Dream or Mission
- Creating Visits That Build Your Relationship
- Making Your Mother's Gifts Your Own
- Writing a Letter to Your Mother Praising the Gifts of Her Life

Finding a Shared Dream or Mission

When you have a shared dream or mission with your mother, it is more than a recreational outing like shopping or having lunch; it is a shared passion, a reason to work together or be together in a very focused way. It gives you months, maybe years of things to do together.

You spend time talking about your dreams, building the excitement, and making it a reality in incremental steps. It puts the focus away from drama, to helping others, to learning something new, to leaving a tangible legacy to the world. It gives your mother a chance to reclaim one of her lost dreams. It shows your children that their dreams are important, too.

TRY THIS

Find a passion that you share with your mother and make a six-month to one-year project out of it. Try some of these things:

PLAN AN EXTENDED VACATION TOGETHER.

Read books about the country, learn the language, cook some of the ethnic foods, make all your travel preparations together.

START A HOME BUSINESS TOGETHER.

You could teach your mother how to use the computer and start a business on the Internet.

SHARE A HOBBY TOGETHER.
One mother and daughter I know like to do crafts, and they are making items for a harvest craft festival. They spend time visiting boutiques, getting ideas about various projects, shopping for materials, and making the crafts together.

GO ON AN ENVIRONMENTAL CRUSADE TOGETHER.
Join an environmental group and volunteer to do fund-raising, speaking, or writing.

WRITE A BOOK OR SCREENPLAY TOGETHER.
You never know—you just might have a great idea for the next mother-daughter chick flick.

START YOUR OWN NONPROFIT ORGANIZATION THAT WILL BENEFIT OTHER WOMEN.
MADD (Mothers Against Drunk Driving) was founded on the collective efforts of mothers who shared the common pain of losing children to drunk drivers. They turned their anger and grief into an organization that has greatly reduced deaths in alcohol-related accidents.

Creating Visits That Build Your Relationship
Why are visits with our families so stressful?—because we don't chunk them down into smaller increments of quality time, but instead try to cram our time together into marathon visits. The right visit can build our relationships, leave us wanting more time with each other. The wrong visit can destroy our relationships, feed the drama, and leave us feeling drained.

Let's understand a few things about visiting our families. First, we decide to brace ourselves and go home. This sets in motion a mild panic attack which gets worse as we prepare for the visit. It's not just the visit that we fear, but the anticipation of the visit and the drama that comes with it, that stresses us out.

The normal routine is we go home and stay for the day or the weekend and we are immediately pushed out of our comfort zone. We eat and drink too much, forget to keep our exercise schedule, forget to give ourselves time alone to collect our thoughts and emotions. If we're just there for dinner, we might get ambushed by those well-meaning relatives, the ones who tell their war stories or want to play "Can you top this?" Everyone's competing—everyone's positioning for power, and we're thinking, "What am I doing here? I'm staying too long!"

Sound like a recipe for disaster? It is. If we're lucky enough to escape without a major conflict, we'll still be drained for days—maybe weeks—and then, the phone campaign starts. All the relatives, sometimes led by our mothers themselves, start gossiping about each other and this goes on until the buzz dies down, and we all brace ourselves for another family visit.

TRY THIS
The next time you go home, try this instead:

ARRIVE ONE HOUR BEFORE DINNER AND VISIT WITH YOUR FAMILY MEMBERS.
The reason you only give yourself an hour is because this is the time it will take to get caught up on current events, what's new, what you're planning to do in the future. If your conversation goes on too long, it could drift into past history and conflict, and you want to avoid this.

KEEP THE CONVERSATION LIGHT AND UPBEAT.
Enjoy dinner with your relatives and tactfully sidestep any conflicts that may come up.

Don't forget to compliment your mother on the food. Be the first one to volunteer to clean the dishes. If you find yourself getting upset about anything, go outside, offer to walk the dog, take a short break to give yourself strength.

LEAVE BEFORE YOU GET ENGAGED IN DRAMA.
An hour after dinner, point to your watch and say that you are expected somewhere else. Tell everyone how nice it was to be with them, and leave.

If you can't do this yourself, assign a designated caretaker, a friend or sibling who will come with you to dinner or call you at your parents' house and remind you it's time to leave.

If you keep the visits short and upbeat, both you and your family will enjoy them more, and you will leave before major problems can occur. When you can learn to do this over a period of years, you will change your relationships with all your relatives and build a calmer legacy for visits in the future.

If you must stay at your family's home for an extended period of time, stick to your routine as much as possible. Rent a car, so you are free to come and go as you please. Go out for coffee or go to the gym to work out. Plan to go to the movies and other outings of your own choosing and invite your family to join in on some of these. Don't expect them to drop everything and entertain you. Encourage them to keep up with their routines as well, to go to their bridge game or bingo night and leave you home alone.

What can often drive you crazy during these visits is the feeling that you're trapped in someone else's home or routine and can't escape. You have to be able to maintain your sense of independence and well-being apart from your family even when you're in their environment. When you put the focus on this, you have more of yourself to share with them.

Making Your Mother's Gifts Your Own

A visiting sensei to my dojo spoke of *borrowing energy*, of us taking the strength of our partner's movement in such a way that we could borrow it, use it, and give it back in our movement. That's what we do when we take our mothers' gifts, make them our own, and express them in our own lives. They become a rich part of our legacy.

One of the greatest gifts Debbie's mother gave her was the ability to detach from everything, the drama and the judgments of other people.

When someone got upset at her or her children, she would calmly ask her family, "If someone is standing there bad-mouthing you, spreading lies about you, how are you going to take it? You can get upset, blow it out of proportion, and get an ulcer—or you can let it go. It takes real character to forgive them, to ask yourself if there is any truth in what they're saying."

Debbie's mother had her practice the art of detachment by watching movies and asking her to suspend her judgment of the "bad guys," to truly understand their motivations for doing things. She'd lean over midway through a movie, and ask, "Are you practicing?" and she and Debbie would get into passionate discussions like whether Han Solo was a good guy or bad guy in *Star Wars*. Her mother's assessment: Han was both, that he acted in his own self-interest, but later came back to save his friends. She explained to Debbie that your environment is stronger than your willpower and that when Han was hanging out with smugglers and thieves, he was acting like one of them.

How has this legacy translated to Debbie's life and her own children? She finds she is better able to pull back from the drama around her and better able to advise her children without becoming emotional. When her own daughter recently called her from college with roommate problems, Debbie was able to say, "We can't do anything about her. What can we do about you? What can you learn here that will help you change your reaction?"

After responding this way, Debbie's daughter was so thankful for her mother's input. "Mother," she said, "it's so nice to be able to call you and get some real advice. Do you know how many mothers would jump on the bandwagon and get their daughters upset at their roommate?" Debbie was touched by her daughter's sentiments, and answered, "Well, you know, darling, that's grandma."

And so it is. When something works in our relationships, it works for generations. Debbie inherited her mother's values of detaching from drama and judgment, and a willingness to give people the benefit of the doubt, and both she and her daughters are benefiting from these values.

TRY THIS

Try journaling about your mother's values and strengths and see if you can identify where you're already borrowing these gifts in your life. Resolve to take new actions which draw on these gifts.

Writing a Letter to Your Mother Praising the Gifts of Her Life

When you find the "aha" in your relationship with your mother, one of the most empowering things you can do is write her a letter praising her gifts. Erin did this and found it to be a powerful affirmation of both her mother and herself.

6/20/94

Dear Mother:

What a wise and wonderful woman you are! But I never realized that until recently when I saw you with fresh eyes.

It excites me to finally understand how many gifts you have given me in my life. And those gifts were always there. I just never really saw them. How grateful I am that you are still alive for me to not only tell you this, but to appreciate you all the more.

My eyes were opened and I thank God for that. He has helped me to see how strong and courageous you are to have grown up under the shadow of your mother and yet to have created some sense of self. Any woman with less internal strength would not have survived.

I sense that as I shed parts of me I have been given that are not me, that you are doing the same. We are becoming more of our true selves and more of the women we were always meant to be. There is a powerful woman inside you that has not fully emerged, and yet I have seen glimpses of her. Who else could have lived through what you have and not withered like a flower in the sun? To me you are a mountain lion—much like myself—brown and lean, beautiful and strong—fearless. A lioness, protective of her cubs, but not overly affectionate.

Now I know—and understand—that you did love me, that you have always loved me, but that you didn't do it in the way that I wanted you to.

I wanted you to pull me into your lap and cuddle me and to smother me in kisses and tell me with words that you loved me. Now I see that you did those very things by teaching me how to think for myself, to ask "why?" to rely on myself, to love nature, to love people.

Your gifts have been there my whole life, and yet I am now just seeing them. It's like unwrapping a Christmas present again and finding a new gift. Or walking down a familiar path and noticing a flower that you had passed by. And it makes me think with stunning clarity, "Wow! It was there all the time."

I went to the mountain to find myself, and I found my mother. My spiritual mother, my physical mother, my internal mother, my eternal mother. My mother, my self. The mother of my soul. She was there all along. I am home. All is well.

Thank you for your gifts. For my life. For teaching me your ways. For your legacy that lives on in me. Thank you most of all, for your love, that I am only now able to receive.

I thank God for you.

Love, Erin

TRY THIS

Write a heartfelt letter like Erin's to your mother, praising the gifts of her life, and you will feel closer to your legacy.

A New Emotional Legacy Is Like Pennies from Heaven

Martha's mother always told her, "You have no regard for money. I would still bend over to pick up a penny." As Martha left her mother's gravesite, she bent over to pick up a 1963 penny, a penny from the year she was twelve years old and her mother was weighing her in on a regular basis. She saw it as a blessing, as something her mother dropped just for her. "It was a miracle, my mother saying, 'I forgive you.' I thought, 'You forgive me, I forgive you.' " To this day Martha continues to find pennies all over the place, even finding one in the ocean when she was snorkeling. She says it is part of her legacy, her special connection with her mother.

For many years pennies from heaven have symbolized the abundance of life, the joy of having beautiful things drop right in our laps. That's what it's like to create a new emotional legacy with your mother and your children. It is a joyful reminder of the goodness and abundance in life that has been available to you all along, if only you will allow it to drop in.

After listening to the beautiful stories of the women who shared their hearts and lives with me, I am more convinced than ever that you can make peace with your mother and have the relationship you want, that it is a blessing there for the taking, a blessing there for the receiving when you are ready. Stay close to the relationship. Never give up. And wait for the pennies. They are truly there.

The Perfect Place for

Mothers and Daughters

Running Out of Time

It took my mother's imminent death to wake me up to the fact that time was running out. I had fooled myself into believing there was always time to settle my problems with her tomorrow. Mother had been diagnosed with cancer and she was given three to six months to live. Suddenly there wasn't time, and I had to make a choice. Did I stay angry at her and refuse to go to her bedside, or did I go, fear and anger and all, and show her, where words often failed, that I loved her?

I waited until the last six weeks of my mother's life to make peace with her . . . that's how stubborn I was. The peace was there all along, if I'd just allowed it to come in. But I was too self-absorbed, too hooked on the drama to rise above it.

When the peace happened, it seemed unreal, easy, effortless. I didn't think I did much, but then I remembered that I did choose to show up and be with her, and that was a lot.

When I walked into her room, I was shocked to see her. My mother had been a big woman, over two hundred pounds, but after the chemotherapy, she was a mere shell of her former self—she'd lost sixty pounds and most of her hair, and her skin had changed to a pale, chalky white. She looked so frail and weak.

You have to understand that my mother was bigger than life to me, not just in her height and physical weight, but her whole persona. She could intimidate me with the slightest look or gesture. She could walk into a room and command the attention of everyone there. She had so much passion for her life missions the only logical choice was to get out of her way and let her go on her crusade. Seeing my mother in her current weakened state was hard, given the context of who she was and the importance she had in shaping my life.

I was jet-lagged from the flight from California, still trying to take everything in—the reality of my mother's illness, my feelings about her death. The nurses, the social worker, the hospice volunteers saw me as this dutiful daughter coming back to be with her mother. They never had a clue that we had experienced so much conflict in our relationship.

So there I was, sitting by her bedside at St. Lawrence Dimondale quietly doing my needlepoint. I'd look up at her every now and then, listening to that awful wheezing sound she was making as she slept. I remember how uncomfortable I felt, not knowing what to do or say, just knowing that this was the place I needed to be.

Mother woke up, took my hand, and said, "It's so good to just have you here, Den." At that moment I looked into her eyes, and I felt such incredible love for her. Before, I only remembered fearing my mother. I knew I was her daughter, and I was supposed to love her, but I think I honestly feared her more than loved her.

But when I looked at her this time, I saw so much more. I saw God's light, that spark of divinity, that spark of holiness in her, and knew instantly that it was in me . . . and my daughters . . . and in all of us. At last I understood that this woman, who had been bigger than life to me, was human and vulnerable, too. My whole life was spent being afraid of this woman, being in awe of her, and I finally saw both her humanity and divinity in one split second.

I sat there thinking about this when I felt it pour over me like waves of soft, warm energy . . . unconditional love. Suddenly, I remembered what I must have felt as a child, but somehow forgot as an adult . . . this was love.

I sighed with relief . . . all things were possible in this place of unconditional love. It had an easiness, a warmth, a flow that I had rarely felt in my life. I took another breath and leaned into it. I cried, kissed her forehead, stroked her hair, and told her just how much she meant to me. I told her I would pass on the stories to her granddaughters and all the wisdom she had taught me. Then I just sat back and felt those waves of love washing over me, taking away the pain, and leaving me with a peace that I had never known before.

When my mother died six weeks later, I was so glad I hadn't missed that moment with her. Since her death, I've had many more moments of reconciliation in which I've been able to embrace the gifts of her life, gifts that often came wrapped in incredible pain. But none of these moments can match that one at her bedside, when all time seemed to stop and I was given a wake-up call about our relationship.

Making peace with her at that moment allowed me to pick up my own life with a renewed sense of purpose, with more longing for finding the same sense of meaningfulness in all my relationships, and a new life mission to share what I learned with other mothers and daughters.

Finally, Sanctuary

Finally, I had found a sanctuary, a safe place where even the most compelling *mama drama* couldn't compete. It came in the quiet, in sitting patiently at my mother's bedside. I knew this was the place to be, far above the petty dramas I had been living with most of my life.

I often share this story in my speeches and one night a woman in my audience came up to me, and asked, "What do you mean you saw 'God's light' in her eyes?" she asked. "Of course you would see light in someone's eyes." I was surprised by this response and a little worried that my God comment had offended her in some way. I did my best to explain an experience that almost defied words. No matter how hard I tried I couldn't quite get through to her that this was real to me, that I had experienced and felt these things and as a result, created a new relationship with my mother in the remaining days of her life.

The next morning, this same woman repeated her question and then shared her story. She told me her mother had never told her she loved her and that when her mother suffered a stroke and went into a coma, the daughter feared her mother would die without the chance to talk to her again. Like me, this woman waited at her mother's bedside, not knowing what to do. Eventually her mother woke up, told her, "I love you," then died. It was as if she couldn't leave this world without telling her daughter she loved her. Needless to say, this meant everything to this woman who had waited her whole life to hear those words from her mother.

As soon as the woman told me this story, I asked, "Did you think you were supposed to see the light in your mother's eyes? Did you feel you might have missed something?" She said yes. I immediately reassured her that her story was miraculous in its own right, and that it happened just the way it was supposed to for her. She had been stuck on my experience as it related to her own healing with her mother.

As she walked away, I couldn't help but feel that there is a moment like this for every mother and daughter, a perfect moment where we truly look at each other and awaken to the fact that the love, the joy, the peace is there for the taking.

The other night, as I was cuddling with my youngest daughter Allison, she put her head on my shoulder, looked up with her dreamy eyes, and said, "Mommy, do you know where the best place for mothers and daughters is?" I looked down at her, hardly believing I was hearing such profoundness from a six-year-old. "Where's that, Allison?" I asked. "Right here, Mommy," she said. I kissed her and joked back, "May I quote you?" (After all, I do have to get permission to use my daughter's material.) She giggled, and said yes.

Allison is only six years old, and she's already had one of her moments with her mother. I hope that both she and her sister will remain open to creating many more such moments with me. I know one thing—I'm committed to creating those moments with them and staying in the best place, the love we share.

Putting Mama Drama to Rest

My mother's favorite place in the whole world was Point Betsie, a beautiful stretch of beach on Lake Michigan in Frankfurt, where the historic Point Betsie lighthouse stands. Reminiscent of the beaches on the East Coast, Point Betsie has that New England feel to it, transporting visitors to another time and location. The gulls swoop lazily over the horizon, and large frothy waves crash against the cement wall that surrounds the lighthouse. Mounds of smooth white sand wait patiently for children young and old alike to come play, and hundreds of small pebbles wash against the shore with each wave that rolls in. Off to the side is an old driftwood log, worn smooth by the water and sun and passersby who care to sit and linger there a while.

It was here, against this scenic backdrop, that my mother came to find sanctuary from the world. She would plop down on the log, look out over the horizon, and just get lost in the hypnotic sounds of Point Betsie—the waves rolling in and out, the cries of the gulls, and the laughter of the boaters and windsurfers on Lake Michigan.

Like Moses on the mountain, she journeyed to this special spot to meet God and have one of her famous chats. Sometimes it was actually more like ranting and other times it was crying slow soft tears or sitting in just plain silence. But no matter what the form, her soul wouldn't rest until she stopped whatever she was doing and spent some time at Point Betsie.

It was here that she screamed out at her parents and husbands for causing her so much pain, here that she worried and prayed and complained about her children, and here that she came to dream about her granddaughters . . . wondering if there would be a cure for Lauren's diabetes, whether or not Taylor would grow up to be a famous artist, chuckling over Meghan's dimples, and marveling at what mysteries Allison, her youngest granddaughter, had in store for her.

Sometimes she'd take her brother Jim with her, and they'd have long talks about their families and life in general, but most of her trips to Point Betsie were made alone, so she could just ponder the things that were troubling her.

She told me that when she was a little girl, she used to just lie down on the ground and do the same thing with the clouds, look up at them, and let them take her away to another place where she could daydream and just be. She said that we kids missed simple pleasures like that because we had so many distractions in our modern lives. I know now that she was right about this, as I look for ways to strip down the complicated life I've created and find joy in simplicity.

Point Betsie was the perfect sanctuary for my mother, the safest place she could go to get off life's merry-go-round and just be herself. It provided the perfect environment to experience the peace she had craved for years but which had eluded her most of her lifetime.

A few months after my mother died, we decided to bury her ashes in the cremation gardens outside her church. Her brother Jim and his wife came up, and all four of the granddaughters were present. Earlier in the day, my sister-in-law and I had taken the girls to Point Betsie to gather some pebbles, sticks, and seagull feathers to bury with the urn. It was our wish that Mother's remains be buried with pieces of her precious sanctuary.

One by one, the granddaughters dropped their treasures into the hole, even little Allison who had just turned one. My daughters still vividly remember this day as the way we really said good-bye to Grandma, and one of their favorite outings in Michigan is a trip to Point Betsie. I have introduced them to their grandmother's sanctuary and they, too, find peace there.

Today, there are times when I yearn to see Point Betsie one more
time, to dig my toes in the wet sand and gather the smooth pebbles at
the shore. I live in one of the most beautiful beach areas of California,
but it is Point Betsie and not the local beaches that calls out to my
soul. I don't feel settled as a woman unless I travel there at least once
a year and walk the same beach that my mother did and sit on the
same smooth log.

The anticipation of going to this place is almost more than I can
bear. It's as if in going there I expect to see my mother sitting on that
log, waiting to have a conversation with me. When I get there I feel a
little bit foolish, because of course she isn't there, but I do feel her
presence, her essence at Point Betsie, and it feeds my soul in a way that
only it can.

The perfect sanctuary for mothers and daughters is a lot like Point
Betsie, a special place that we share together safely harbored from
life's storms. In truth, this sanctuary can exist anywhere—in the warmth
of a hug, in the compassion of the moment, in the peace that comes
from sharing the best we have to give as mothers and daughters. For
me, it came at my mother's bedside in a nursing home, when I faced
her death and felt the strong piercing presence of unconditional love.
And it has come in looking at my own daughters' eyes and realizing that
my mother's legacy continues in them.

Making peace with my mother has been the most incredible, freeing
journey I've taken, because I now carry the radiance and love that
comes from settling my life on the deepest level. I miss Mother terri-
bly. I praise the gifts of her life. And I release her to Point Betsie to chat
with God some more.

Resources

Communication

To understand more about the power of your words and the need to choose them wisely, read Rabbi Joseph Telushkin's book, *Words That Hurt, Words That Heal,* William Morrow & Company, 1996. To find out more about Dr. Ralph Kellogg's seminars on color-coded communication, contact him at (760) 741-2530.

Eating Disorders Information

To order your free Eating Disorders Bookshelf Catalogue, featuring W. Charisse Goodman's book, *The Invisible Woman: Confronting Weight Prejudice in America,* and other books, contact Gurze Books at 1-800-756-7533 or E-mail: www.gurze.com.

Fat Burning Diet

To order Jay Robb's book, *The Fat Burning Diet* and a full line of nutritional products and supplements, contact Jay Robb Enterprises at 1-800-862-8763, fax (760) 634-5490.

Goddess Tape

To order your goddess tape, contact Fred Stemen at 1-800-204-9766.

Memos from Mom

To order a set of 8 Memos from Mom doorknob hangers, contact Jan Connors, owner of Art & Soul, at (760) 634-6898 (phone and fax).

Kama Sutra Box

To get a mail order catalogue for the Kama Sutra Weekender Kit, as well as other massage oils, lotions, and creams, call the toll free number 1-800-216-3620, offered by The Kama Sutra Company, Westlake Village, CA.

Mentoring

To form a Mastermind group, read Napoleon Hill's classic book, *Think and Grow Rich*, Ballantine/Fawcett, 1996.

To form a Princessa Roundtable, contact Erin Thomas Palmeter c/o The Palmeter Group, E-mail: 105120.2310@compuserve.com. Erin is the creator of The Princessa Workshop and Princessa Roundtables based on the book *The Princessa: Machiavelli for Women*, by Harriet Rubin, Currency Doubleday, 1997.

Time-Management System

To order *The 7 Habits Organizer*, call Franklin Covey at 1-800-863-1492.

Weight Loss

Lindora Medical Clinics is a medically based weight management company that offers safe medical weight-loss and weight-maintenance services to their patients under the supervision of physicians and nurses who are trained experts in the field of health and nutrition. They have developed the Lean for Life™ weight loss/maintenance program for people who wish to lose five to five hundred pounds and break free from the childhood scripts that keep them struggling with their weight.

Lindora offers some excellent books: *Lean for Life*, by Cynthia Stamper Graff, with Jerry Holderman (Griffin Publishing Company), and *Bodypride: An Action Plan for Teens: Seeking Self-Esteem and Building Better Bodies*, by Cynthia Stamper Graff, Janet Eastman, and Mark C. Smith (Griffin Publishing Company).

For more information about Lindora and their products and programs, call their toll-free number, 1-888-LEAN4LIFE, or visit their web site: www.leanforlife.com.

Denise McGregor is an award-winning professional speaker, workshop leader, and columnist for San Diego's *Living Better* magazine. Known for her lively conversational style, Denise has been featured in dozens of articles and broadcasts nationwide, including *Cosmopolitan* magazine, Lifetime Television's "New Attitudes," and ABC-TV's "The View." Denise has a Master's degree in Guidance and Counseling, and training in the martial art Aikido, which have contributed greatly to her understanding of relationship dynamics. She lives in La Costa, California, with her two daughters.